MAPPING
THE INVISIBLE
EU-ROMA GYPSIES

edited by lucy orta

black dog publishing
london uk

DEDICATION

We dedicate this book to Professor Claudio Marta, anthropologist, scholar of immigration, racism, and intolerance, friend of Roma and Sinti and activist for human rights, who passed away on 26 December 2008, at the age of 58.

Claudio Marta was professor of Anthropology and Interethnic Relations at the University of Napoli 'L'Orientale', Italian member of the 'Committee of Experts on Roma and Travellers' of the Council of Europe, and scientific expert and mentor for the cultural cooperation project European Roma Mapping (EU-Roma).

In his decades of professional activity, he was distinguished in the area of anthropological and social research. He was a member of numerous scientific international commissions.

Working with intense passion to bring to light the historic roots of Roma and Sinti culture, Professor Marta was an important and active figure, and a protagonist of peaceful dialogue.

Colleagues in academia all over the world respect the excellence of his research, the quality of his publications and the legacy he has left. Everyone, in scientific and humanitarian arenas, who had the great fortune to know Professor Marta, appreciated his great gift of humanity.

With all our gratitude to his support, his affection and with sadness.

EU-Roma

CONTENTS

PREVIOUS PAGE
Kalderasha in Camp Boario, Rome 1986.
Photographic archive of Aldo Udorovic.

FOREWORD

Alexander Valentino and Lucy Orta

European Roma mapping stemmed from the need to know more about the precarious living conditions of the Romani across Europe. Awareness, we believe, is an absolutely necessary first step towards an auspicious change in the Roma condition. The EU-Roma project is an attempt to expose the current situation, through an open dialogue with Roma across Europe, and this publication brings together a small fragment of our research.

It is estimated that there are over ten million Roma currently in Europe and that they have been leaving their identity on this continent for more than 800 years; thus, the Roma are the only people who can truly boast the title of European citizen. The absence of political representatives and a national state have only accentuated the condition of strong social marginalisation. The Roma have been subjects of repression, segregation and extermination generally living in the suburbs of the city, in run-down areas, in places that resemble the shantytowns, slums and favelas of Africa and South America. With the increasing gentrification of the historic centres of European cities, the Roma risk being pushed even further to peripheral areas, becoming ever more marginalised and excluded from productive urban environments: the 8th district of Budapest, the district of Sulukule in Istanbul, resettled beyond the Grande Raccordo Anulare in Rome, are among the more shocking examples of this phenomenon that we have chosen to illustrate.

Despite the extreme difficulties, the Romany resist, apparently passively, planning and employing strategies for survival, to continue their existence in the countries that they retain as their places of abode. The *campi nomadi* in Italy were born in this way, the roadside camps for *les gens de voyage* in France, the village for *zigeuner* in Germany, the *Tzigani* quarters in Greece or in Serbia, the occupation of abandoned factories, in workers apartments emptied by the closure of factories in Hungry. Their settlements resist when they find themselves in non-secure areas, near or indeed inside rubbish dumps, beside working or disused and polluted industrial estates. Their communities border prisons, canals, and psychiatric hospitals. They are tolerated under the bypasses of highways, on the banks of rivers and in many other places where they remain hidden—invisible—and where the *Gaje* (non-Roma) have no self-interest.

There exist many worthy non-profit organisations who attempt to help the Roma, financing enterprise projects, social inclusion, cultural workshops and school programs, but very few which are managed directly by the Romani communities. Instead, they are almost always excluded from the funding networks, marginalised and given secondary or third order roles such as the cleaning of the settlements or school transportation in guise of collaboration. Over the twenty months of the EU-Roma cooperation, the mistrust of these organisations and of local institutions has been significant: the entrance to the Roma camps Castel Romano in Rome, as in Rahova in Bucharest have been barred. We, and the students we worked with, have encountered serious problems with the forces of law and order: for the project inauguration in an Italian Roma camp, police in riot gear sequestrated our documents, we were requested not to interact with the inhabitants, nor to photograph or record in any way the police actions, for the entire length of the operation. One particular example we wish to underline took place in Monachina Rome where, after our visit and discussions with the community, police arrested 10 men of working age with the accusation of connecting illegally to the electrical current; a decision clearly aimed at compromising the already difficult economy of the community composed of 120 people, who after years of illegal use of the current, with our help had requested a legal connection from both the local council and electricity company.

These episodes, beyond their intrinsic gravity, have been documented amongst many others because they are indicative of the objective difficulty in facing the "Romani question".

By consolidating a European network of architects, artists, designers, urban planners, sociologists and activists under the umbrella or EU-Roma, we are convinced that a greater awareness of the cultural, environmental, social and historical context, despite the dire problems of daily existence, represents a fundamental step forward towards the overcoming of *Gaje* prejudicial behaviour on a socio-cultural level. The decision to participate in a pan-European funded project has been motivated by the considerations outlined above and allows us, from this small presumption, to provoke and put into place new policies and begin developing solutions that can be shared and adopted where the dignified survival of Roma communities is at great risk.

EU-ROMA

Gabi Scardi

Born from converging interests regarding the Roma/Gypsy people, the EU-Roma European project has evolved as a sensitive interdisciplinary course, a collective platform of experiences and research.

During over two years of work, EU-Roma has attracted participants from Italy, Greece, the United Kingdom, Romania, Turkey and Serbia: heterogeneous figures from a professional point of view and diverse as regards individual sensibilities, though united in a fundamental orientation, all sharing a sense of involvement in collective life.

The elements shared by the participants and what has bound the project together consist in a decided openness to exchange and attributing to culture an active and socially responsible role. The EU-Roma project was born from the belief that inflexible, or even openly discriminatory, positions, which even today are frequent with regards to minorities, are the result of a distance, of a desire not to know or see others, of not recognising in others that which makes us similar; and that this insensitivity is the expression of intellectual conformism and of the tendency to passively adapt to intentionally superficial social discourses. The project was born with the intention of opposing this attitude, inviting broader awareness based on openness and contact, on direct and shared experiences. Upon this basic affinity, EU-Roma has developed as a form of shared activity. Moreover, in the field of research, what forcefully emerged was the difference of the participants' background contexts.

It is no coincidence that the initiative was devised by architect Alexander Valentino in Italy, a country which at this moment is experiencing a phase in which social perception and policies tied to welcoming and assimilating foreigners in society has grown more and more restricted and limited. The activity has been carried out according to different modalities.

EU-Roma has given rise to study and divulgation phases with reunions, public presentations, days dedicated to forums, and conferences with broad themes. The practical and experience aspects of the project have been characterised by vitality and collective intervention. The analytical level, whose scientific value did not hinder participants from reaching, at times, emotional intensity, crossed paths with the theoretical level, underlying the entire initiative.

The different phases witnessed the involvement of various reference points and different types of public. Among the shared activities there have been visits to the Roma residential areas, days spent together in cooperative activities such as preparing the dinner and party organised by Maria Papadimitriou in the Aliveri settlement, the organisation of workshops and seminars by LAN (Laboratorio di Architettura Nomade) in Italy, exhibitions and presentations in public galleries in Bucharest, at the Muzeul Taranului Roman (Museum of Traditional Culture) and the MNAC (Museum of Contemporary Art) coordinated by Catalin Berescu, and in London at RIBA (Royal Institute for British Architects) and Autograph by Lucy Orta.

Moreover, EU-Roma has constituted the germinative nucleus of a series of projects aimed at developing beyond its own extent, in an assigned artistic field.

The Roma people constitute, as a whole, an extremely vulnerable group of inhabitants in our countries. The Roma are united by the fact they live, in most of Europe, in precarious situations; even today, their existence is relegated to the outskirts of cities and emarginated by collectivity, neglected or even denied laws that regulate social cohabitation.

Yet these communities tend to be perceived as a threat. The individuals are fragile; their uneasiness is evident; their position in society is nevertheless residual, regardless of the economic role they play. In many cases, their lives are spent in a sense of disorientation and awaiting, which prove to be ordeals. The energy and brutality with which they are still refused, after centuries of discrimination and, in many cases, slavery, in many parts of the world, is blatantly disproportionate.

The image of this population is mainly the result of insinuations and generalisations; the dangerousness attributed to them has to do in part with the reality of people who are the children of a history of exclusion, of abandonment, of scandalous poverty, and therefore extraneous to the lifestyle that unites the majority of citizens. But the perception of this dangerousness is amplified by a lack of knowledge.

An irrational intolerance is joined with the desire to not know and not distinguish and, simply, to avoid any issue. In fact, the Roma are mainly known by superficial information, distorted by prejudice and stereotypes that lead one down the wrong track. Often this information is artfully constructed by populist governments intent on singling out an enemy upon which to catalyse with excuses social tensions that would otherwise necessitate regulation through more complex social interventions.

Rarely are the Roma people are considered analytically, in their extreme heterogeneity, in their layers and internal hierarchy. Rarely do we understand their cultural peculiarities and their complexity, due to the geographical dispersion and encounters with different social contexts.

Instead, they are attributed with generic notions of "non-complying" persons: non-placeable, indefinable, and more generally uncontrollable; destabilising, therefore with their very presence, with respect to social structures that play on the need for norms and stability and which automatically involve the refusal of what is different. Destabilising even more so in a system that declares itself as being global but which in reality remains based on an facile feeling of belonging and its opposite, the impulse to take refuge in micro-units and to exclude all that which does not directly refer to the main group.

It must be said that, even though the Roma society constitutes a microcosm that is as diverse as the society of its context, in turn the Roma tend to respond to the outside political scene that marginalises them from every point of view by activating protection and self-defense mechanisms; acknowledging themselves in communities based upon strong internal conventions and discouraging therefore openness and change. Precisely because they are scattered across the world, the Roma, like other minorities, also tend to cling onto the culture of family relations and ancestral customs. Their settlements, places marked off by imposed perimeters, thus become a special-statute territory both for those who live inside and for those who look on from the outside. At the same time, within their own universe, the Roma tend to split up into groups, and their composite, fragmented, temporary consistency, tenaciously attached to details and traditions only partially shared, makes it difficult for them to cooperate and reach common goals. This therefore makes them even more fragile.

Generally speaking, we may assert that the Roma, despite their internal differences, represent the paradigm of those who aim to maintain their typicalness and autonomy, without however having to give up a place in public discourse. The reality of Roma/Gypsy people emerged as a paradigm of the right to belong to a society, and not to belong to it at the same time. And of the challenging possibility, for our society, to unite without blurring, and to separate without dividing.

This would place this population in a position that does not belong to the geopolitical context of reference, nor is it extraneous to it, but rather it entails a complex co-belonging. A ubiquitous position, full of potential, but also profoundly subversive, able to overturn the definitions and conventions upon which many populist systems of today base themselves. Giorgio Agamben in *The Coming Community*, 1990, elaborates the idea of a complete and unconditional, "being-such", or more precisely of "the belonging itself"; of singularities that would represent a "belonging without belonging" that would function without any specific attribute or property that usually defines belonging to a certain set or group.

As regards this position defined by Agamben, Suzana Milevska, an art and visual culture theorist, asked herself at a recent conference organised by the IKT and held at the Museum Kiasma of Helsinki: "My question is actually how one negotiates such 'belonging without belonging', without abiding to the particular requirements of belonging, and whether potentiality of not-to-belong is also an issue of negotiation." She brought as an example a protest initiated by a Roma group in front of a cinema in Skopje, Macedonia, which was showing the film *The Shutka Book of Records*. In the film, the Roma is exclusively represented as a dispossessed person. The protest expressed the feeling of a group accustomed to earthly pain, but always reluctant to accept the mortifying leveling of their image into a stereotype that turns them only and without distinction into a group of "victims". Instead, she says they are people aware of their own values and own potentials, of the surrounding socio-political context, able to actively reclaim their right to share, to social distribution, to having their collective and individual identity acknowledged.

The discourse on belonging and on the value of nomadism in so far as being a philosophical and aesthetic category, in so far as a paradigm, could be broadly extended. We need only think of the enlightened comments of Deleuze and Guattari, of Rosi Braidotti, but also of Irit Rogoff; and, even before, of the seminal role that, with respect to twentieth century art, the Situationist Movement had, in which nomadism was a fundamental concept, concentrated with meaning, with the idea of freedom and self-determination, in the refusal of a capitalist production system and accumulation of goods, in the rediscovery of a spirit of adventure on the part of the individual in an urban setting. The Situationist artist Pinot

Gallizio had himself photographed with a pair of earrings that portrayed him as the "King of the Gypsies". It was also Gallizio who pushed the architect Constant to embark upon the design of New Babylon, a nomadic and modular city: a titanic undertaking Constant worked on for 25 years, and which constituted the germinative nucleus of Radical Architecture.

Without going beyond these ideas, we should note that referring to the idea of nomadism—so often incarnated by the Roma irregardless of and in any event well beyond the actual itinerant nature of their existence in modernity—means moving towards an attention that is always vigil and a critical reconsideration of reality and of the world we live in; a world in which change is inscribed like a constant condition, in a continual game of permanence, reproduction, and metamorphosis.

The concrete reality experienced by the Roma in most European countries speaks however of tragic paradox: that of a people who are not allowed to take root and who are instead forced to live upon the discards of non-nomadic citizens, often refusing a stable and regular lifestyle; but at the same time they are hindered in their movement. This is one of the most significant paradoxes of our global age: a period in which there is a degree of motion that up until a few years ago was unthinkable and which can be attributed to, on the one hand, the ever vaster waves of immigration, and on the other, a "symbolic class" made up of a growing number of persons who, having singled out in mobility a merit and a lifestyle, find themselves as globe trotters by choice or for work. Even taking a trip is not the same for everyone, and there exists categories of people for whom this means challenging restrictions, control, and policies of exclusion. At times it seems that geopolitical confines, paradoxically increasingly elastic and guarded, are more open to goods, which circulate frenetically, than to people, who move more and more in a sort of probation.

In this sense the EU-Roma project is a tool of communication, a channel for a critical outlook and an idea of openness, of inclusion, of cultural interaction. It expresses, in short, the perspective of sustainable citizenship, in a world in which each person may find his or her own space by moving beyond the condition of marginalisation and need. A world that has as its goal the long-term application of concrete and precise strategies of transformation. This entails a difficult metamorphosis, which may encounter resistance, which takes place in phases that alternate between acceleration and slowing down, which at times must be faced urgently. It seems that the Roma situation represents, among these emergencies, one of the most alarming.

What characterises the EU-Roma project is the attempt to apply the Roma situation to an attitude aimed at understanding and questioning, beginning with different points of view, though always extremely similar. This project was born from the desire to live in relation to others; it was an opportunity to participate in a precise context, understood in its peculiarities. A way of drawing attention to a complex situation that is often demagogically exploited, and of formulating hypotheses of development, of change. The field of research singled out was intended as practiced territory, and society as conducted reality; and as a place of the intersection of individual and collective sensibilities, as the seat of necessity, but also of potentials that resound for those who know how to listen.

This situation of the Roma is one that can welcome artists incited by the idea of experiencing themselves and the world. Artists alien to that fear of what is new and which, often falsely alimented, may assume the most ancient forms of discrimination; but instead, attracted by the potentials of a future that is as yet unpredictable. Artists who know how to put at stake an empathetic outlook which in differences sees the value of investigating and which is aware of the distance that separates and of the possible difficulties of approach, but which is able to express something else by the analytical attitude of the scholar and by the attitudes of assistance and emergency with which the Roma are normally approached.

An outlook that is able to renounce facile dichotomies and does not fear entering sensitive areas, negotiating on unstable lands, able to single out the similarities that bind us and respect differences; which does not fear extreme closeness; which, actually, searches for nearness, wholeness, singularity, knowing that individual identity and collective identity do not constitute monolithic and unchangeable wholes predetermined by places of origin. Instead they are shimmering, contingent, constantly redefined, and are always enriched thanks to encounters and influences. "I can write only if I'm able to let myself be invaded by the life of others", declared some time ago the Israeli writer David Grossman, an artist of words, of interior probing, of visions. It is no coincidence that Grossman uses the word "invade": a strong term, which speaks of mistrust, hardship, resistance, anxiety of certainties endangered by the encounter with "the extraneous to the self". It is also no coincidence that he expressed the need for this invasion, the opportunities, the wealth of a future innate to this openness to change. It exemplifies a vision and, opposing the modest belief that holds us immobile, sustains that alternatives exist and are possible, if we have the courage to disentangle ourselves from the social stereotypes upon which the culture of separation bases itself and instead face reality with broad strategies.

The more tangible and immediate outcome of the project consists in, besides a production of knowledge partially summed up in this publication, a few works and interventions that are specifically artistic. In particular, Catalin Berescu and Lucy Orta created, as part of the EU-Roma project, the *Roma Preview Pavilion*, presented at the Biennale di Architettura di Venezia in 2008: a series of tents adorned with textile applications that evoke the visible characteristics typical of Roma clothing and furnishing. They thus brought to the forefront the issue of the home, man's primary need, a fundamental constituent element of individual and collective identity, as well as a veritable emergency for many Roma: forced into settlements that become sites of exclusion, of submission and exasperation, at times even in those following brutal clearings.

The tents made by artist Lucy Orta were distributed, alone or in small settlements, in a random and spontaneous way, throughout the Biennale Gardens, among and across the Pavilions, temporarily installing them where a National Pavilion showed its willingness to host them. In short, they constituted an evident metaphor of the present and constant condition of the Roma, adaptable out of necessity, itinerant out of lack of alternatives more than by choice, without any certain rights: communities that exist in an interstitial and dependent condition with respect to those who "host" them.

The term "preview", on the other hand, speaks of a gaze that looks forward. It speaks of being located in a present that is always temporary, rooted in lived experience and in acquired usages, and aimed at the future at the same time, through planning, anticipation, and the ability to dream. During the Biennale *Roma Preview Pavilion* caught the attention of viewers, allowing them to begin conversing and exchanging opinions, each of which represented a precious opportunity to reconsider the issue of the right to a place, to an acknowledged identity, to fair social sharing.

In the EU-Roma project, there is also the project Lucy + Jorge Orta, *Wandering*: a video installation composed of four projections in which a woman dances to the notes of traditional music, making wide lavishly colourful skirts with huge flower prints happily whirl around, created especially by the artist in the workshops of the London College of Fashion.

This is a subjective but culturally rooted act, a romantic ritual, bursting with energy, with a sense of joyous faith. Thus the work evokes a shared aesthetic and a collective ritual, the strong attitude of the Roma culture with regards to music and dance. What is striking here are the gestures and concentration of circular, quick or slow, spontaneous or poetical movements, always changing without losing rigour; at times the motion of the dancer is ironically affected. They express the flowing, the virtually infinite meeting of courses, of acts, of destinies, of stories; narrating; time that passes and survives, the afterwards, beyond ruptures and discontinuity. But also modernity that does not erase tenaciously rooted habits. If the nomadism attributed to the Roma today tends to become a pretext to deprive them of the possibility of settling in one place and establishing bonds, seeing *Wandering* is like walking down the road of the history of the Roma people, repeating their wanderings by recuperating the most vital and fecund aspects.

Instead, for Maria Papdimitriou, art may be understood as a cultural production for a new neighbourhood policy. A keen sensibility with regards to the Roma has led her to enhance a few concrete aspects of the Roma/Gypsy way of life and aesthetics with long-term projects, like T.A.M.A., *Temporary Autonomous Museum for All*.

The artist has always given preference to the idea of personal exchange, of the group, of collaboration, of teamwork. A direct and in-depth understanding of the Roma, a creative participation and empathetic attitude able to dissipate tensions lie at the heart of her interventions.

As part of the EU-Roma project, Papadimitriou set up a series of study moments including a conference and encounters with local authorities and the media, as well as moments of encounter and real and direct understanding of the reality of the Roma residing in Greece. Among the initiatives there have been itineraries through different settlements in Greece, in the region of Tessalia around the city of Volos, which with its university became the epicentre of the project. A few days were used for a full-immersion in the everyday life of the Aliveri community. Once again, what emerged was the issue of housing, the home as discriminating factor and dream of stability, but also as the subject of extraordinary abilities to plan and build. What also came forth was the incredible ability to adhere to places: perhaps in so far as historically itinerant, the Roma people know best how to understand and make the most of the territory they find themselves living in. The survival tactics they have developed in Greece foresee, among other things, self-construction, recuperation and recycling, restoration of found objects, door-to-door selling. All these are non-invasive activities, interstitial with respect to the existing social context. Though among opportunities and opportunism, among contradictory tensions to essentiality and exhibitionism, among legitimate reclaiming and solutions that exploit the flexibility of the norms, up to cases of illegality, these people may indicate a path to social transformation aimed at a more sustainable life that is less subject to the co-action of consumer systems and accredited conventions. We may attribute to them a workshop value with respect to the instances of moderation and attention to the resources that are widespread in today's world.

With the EU-Roma project, Papadimitriou also conceived of a big feast that involved the cooperation of the Alivieri inhabitants and the EU-Roma participants. All the phases that led up to the party were shared. The feast concept was interpreted by Papadimitriou as a ritual moment but also as hospitality, the greatest openness of the community, and therefore a break in habits; a moment of joy, in which everyone is welcome: the metaphor of a fuller, happier, and more comprehensive existence.

Regarding the Roma, Maria Papadimitriou is able to grasp their humanity, the necessity, the individual stories, the ability to communicate, the tiniest common denominators that relate to herself and to us; and the principles—spontaneous but tenaciously rooted—of a self-determined aesthetics, informal but equipped with a precise code involving sight and sense. "I who am always the other", wrote the philosopher Jean-Luc Nancy in his book *The Inoperable Community*. And so Papadimitriou, who in the certainty of the existence of an 'other', of other than our own everyday conventions, finds the possibility for confrontation and the guarantee of a democratic society that is happily inclusive, able to assure rights without asking for leveling in exchange.

EU-Roma is a moment of direct confrontation among various persons on the meaning of making culture by feeling part of a period. We live in the world, and it awaits us. Making art and culture cannot be a punctiform, intermittent manifestation of formal evidence or events; rather, the ability to face today with all effort possible, to interpret it, to re-orientate it, to imbue it with a sense of ever-new necessary change. The worksite of democracy never stops.

The aesthetic actions of the artists mentioned and of others who participated in the EU-Roma project, the notion of culture upon which the project is nurtured, are based upon a conscious outlook upon reality, upon a position of attention and responsibility: a position that is an invitation to keep our eyes wide open. One that, above all, does not allow us to turn our backs on complexity, on its unhappiness, its worthlessness, on its emergencies. And it appears to us that the Roma situation represents one of these emergencies.

Gabi Scardi is an independent curator and art critic based in Milan, Italy.

THE PURE PRODUCTS GO CRAZY

WHY ARE WE INTERESTED IN ROMA CULTURE AND SETTLEMENTS?

Yorgos Tzirtzilakis

The culture of the Roma people, but also their settlements, form part of the demonised—and mythicised—nomadic experiences which challenge some of the foundations of Western civilisation and our entrenched views and categorisations. Being the 'unknown' that threatens the 'known', they are pushed to the margins of society, to the outskirts of cities and to a kind of topography of the evil. They are seen as a literal threshold between modes of life and habitation; as a prime target for the mythologies of the 'other', the sinister.

Although the modernist tradition does have some examples of designs for Roma settlements, we cannot really claim that these attempts make up a fully useable corpus. Their weakness lies in the difficulties and the inconsistencies of processing the 'different'. I shall stop at two of the most interesting projects which also represent two different approaches, one utopian and one pragmatic utopian, and reflect the personalities of the individuals behind them.

It is a known fact that the Situationists took an interest in the experience of Gypsy camps, especially during the famous 1956 meeting in Alba. The painter Giuseppe Pinot Gallizio, who was a native of that part of northern Italy, was already known for his campaigning for the rights of Roma people. In December 1956, during the meetings of the Imaginist Bauhaus in Alba, Giuseppe Pinot-Gallizio took Constant Nieuwenhuys to a Gypsy camp, and Constant's models of this encampment became the first in a series of maquettes of an ideal city called "New Babylon where, under one roof, with the aid of moveable elements, a shared residence is built; a temporary, constantly remodelled living area; a camp for nomads on a planetary scale."[1]

Indeed, in his Design for a Gypsy Camp of the following year, Constant works on the idea of a flexible radial structure which employs lightweight elements and a system of moveable partitions that allow various layouts to suit the inhabitants' needs. It may seem like a paradox, but this maquette of stainless steel, aluminium, Plexiglas and oil on wood that was addressed to the Roma population of northern Italy inaugurated the explosive mythology of the post-war era's most popular utopian megamachine which was aimed at hosting transients and generating ambiances. Constant mobility and playfulness, neo-primitivism and the indefinite, certain references to Marcuse and science fiction are some of the main concepts behind the design of this elevated megastructure which eschews functionalism. In this way nomadism shifts from habitation to the changeable nature of the architectural language—and thus brings to mind what Deleuze and Guattari once wrote about Kafka: "a Gypsy of his own language"—and exacerbates the twofold act of deterritorialisation and re-territorialisation.[2]

Four years later, in 1961, and as part of France's post-war reconstruction, the architect Georges Candilis becomes the government's advisor on "Gypsy architecture" as he defines it himself: "During the war in Albania I had my first close look at a Gypsy settlement, and I was greatly impressed by the way of living of this free and unusual people. Later, I was able to study their settlements in the South of France and mostly in Spain. These are semi-nomadic populations; they spend the winter at the settlements, and the summer travelling around."[3]

Based on this assumption, Candilis designed a settlement on the outskirts of Avignon, with the emphasis on the identity and the special character of its inhabitants. "It was a very hard problem", he notes. "The notion of ownership is entirely different in these people. The houses are inhabited in turn by different families. My design comprised four rings of 20 apartments each, a school and a social/cultural centre. The open space at the centre of each ring was a courtyard—the common lounge…. The old trucks and carts in which they travelled became one with the houses during the winter. In the end, after 20 years without maintenance these buildings fell to ruins and were torn down."

Strangely enough, this last bitter comment seems to reflect the inevitable fate of most Roma settlements and the temporary character of any such project. However, we could see this kind of failure as a critique on the part of those who are called upon to inhabit the models of organised habitation imposed on them. I do not know of any longer-lived examples, nor the extent to which recent architecture and contemporary art were able to approach such a subaltern culture shaped by the special relations of both dependence and autonomy, under the weight of a dipole of "knowledge/power". Through this peculiar dipole, the Western gaze construes the Roma culture as an entity, but at the same time it colonises and confines it.

In any case, what we must admit is that our 'images' and perceptions of the Roma people are often shaped either by the institutions and devices of authority (even when they maintain a social *mien*) or by their representations in Western imagination. It is natural for such a perception to cover only some aspects of the character of Roma settlements and populations, hence we tend to manage more our own problems than those of the 'others'.

In this sense, the mediation of artists, anthropologists and architects in the processes of representation of the Roma culture cannot but be questionable and problematic.[4] Nevertheless, we must admit that the conversion of all those 'local' experiences into a common ground for interdisciplinary approach and action does not reflect only a necessary attempt to start a dialogue and remove the marginalisation; it has also to do with reorienting the practices of habitation, revising the stereotypical evaluations of underdevelopment, of the irrational and the formless, and rethinking the modern approaches to design and knowledge.

In 1939, the famous text on "Avant-Garde and Kitsch" by the American art critic Clement Greenberg shed light on the context in which modernity dealt with any cultures and artistic experiences outside the scope of abstraction.[5] This reading of Greenberg

Georges Candilis, Housing for
Gypsies in Avignon, France 1961.

helps us to see the subtle attitude of High Modernism towards
anything outside the abstract structures of modern thought, often
rejecting all those annoying constructs, fragments and hybrids
derived from the fusion between modern tradition and traditional
society. It was under the same criterion that it expressed its
interest in local traditions.

Only a few years earlier, Henry-Russell Hitchcock and Philip
Johnson had organised the International Style exhibition at the
Museum of Modern Art (MoMA) in New York, in which they
compiled and classified the traits of global simulated modernity.
The distinction between high and low culture was now elevated
into a universal axiom, and abstraction became the general
iconic symbol and cultural trademark of Western modernism.
Everything outside this universal language was seen as inferior–or
exotic–and all non-Western, peripheral cultures as minor ones or
as mere "consumers of the modern".

The verse of the American poet William Carlos Williams,
used by James Clifford in his introduction to *The Predicament
of Culture*, fits perfectly here: "The pure products of America/
go crazy" (Spring and all, 1923).[6] Indeed, around that time,
folkloristics, anthropology and ethnography–above all French
anthropology and that new field that Clifford describes as
a fusion of ethnography and Surrealism–begin to focus on a
'lower' folklore material. I can cite as an example the little-
recognised Greek folklorist Angeliki Hatzimichali, who devoted
many years to the systematic study of the folk culture of the
Greek islands as well as of nomadic mountain populations
such as the Sarakatsani.[7] Seen as a foreign minority by the local
populations, the Sarakatsani who came down with their herds
from the mountains to spend the winters in the plains were
treated just as we treat the Roma today: with distrust and

fear. So we do need to point out that her research helped to diminish prejudice. I am not suggesting in any way that we can compare, or even contrast, the views of Greenberg with those of Hatzimichali. I am only citing the latter's folklorist readings—which easily show her intention to legitimate and provide continuity—as an example of a different approach to minor forms of folk culture and to the makeshift constructions of flexible living and mobile habitation, which High Modernism treated awkwardly, if not disdainfully.

The reflective journeys of Claude Lévi-Strauss into the savage "cold societies" (which produce little entropy and tend to retain their original state) and the doubt against the worn-out Western rationalism, which was precipitated by the dramatic end of World War Two, were to broaden and radically transform the geographies of the gaze.[8] These events led the Dutch architect Aldo van Eyck to seek the existential meaning of communal life among the indigenous cultures and the settlements of northern Africa, and the Austrian-American architect Bernard Rudofsky to explore the universal anthropological aspect of the various forms of primitive and spontaneous habitation; in 1964 he organised at the MoMA a seminal exhibition with the emblematic title *Architecture Without Architects*. In the same cultural context, the Greek architect Aris Konstantinidis introduced the culture of mobility in his *Elements of Self-Awareness* (1938–1973), for a "true architecture": the photos and drawings of greengrocers' stalls, awnings stretched over the benches and carts of travelling peddlers, timber-and-thatch huts, tents and sheep-pens exalt the attractions of local character and outdoor living.

So how can we talk today about the nomadic Roma culture, when everything we know about it has been shaped mostly by our own Western civilisation? How can we define this culture and follow its current transformations? What is it that correlates Roma objects, lifestyles and modes of habitation with a series of contemporary artistic and architectural practices? These questions lie at the core of every recent approach, such as that of Maria Papadimitriou, the "Eu-Roma" interdisciplinary programme or the resourceful documentation of Roma settlements in Thessaly by the students of the Department of Architecture, University of Thessaly in Greece. Yet one issue remains unresolved, as pointed out by Maria Karamitsopoulou as she sums up her experience from working with a public institution: "We have had enough of the various programmes for the unfeasible social integration of the Roma; of the failure to establish unmediated communication with their social base which lives under the conditions of increased exclusion and destitution; of the difficulty of setting up a thread of actions and communication which would join the individual projects and add effectiveness and consistency."

It would be foolish and useless to use tricks to cover up these questions which take us back to the root of the problem. The Roma culture is one that attracts and alarms us at the same time. I should stop at this as a major obstacle, although one key change in the approach to a civilisation of this kind was achieved once we stopped looking at it as an aesthetic or exotic phenomenon and began to examine it from the viewpoint of cultural anthropology. This change has not eradicated that element which fascinates and scares us at the same time: something familiar to which we feel close, and something

unfamiliar and uncanny which looks alien to us. This tormenting vacillation and wavering is something we all know but find hard to admit.

There are various explanations one could proffer for this contradiction. The one I would go for is that many of the current traits of Roma communities are fiercely debated, in one way or another, in the context of contemporary theory. These traits are quite familiar, and I do not need to enumerate them. For example, the notion of temporariness, or, better, the threat of permanent temporariness in post-Fordist and post-industrial societies is something we recognise in Roma lifestyles. So it is possible that we discern in these cultures the allegory and the projection of a sinister future, but also a prior human condition which we are no longer able to process and understand. Through our erratic study of these scattered communities we see some durable traits which have survived and have us worried, while at the same time some other traits continue to fascinate us.

The 'picture' of the Gypsies' ceaseless and fiery eroticism with the passionate songs, the ecstatic dances, the adventures, the feasts, the duels, the hint of magic practices and the mythologies of flight and carefree natural life is one that exerts an undying attraction on us. *Carmen* by George Bizet and Prosper Mérimée, 1845—which in turn has elements from Pushkin's *Tsygany* (*Gypsies*)—sums up this stereotype in the most complete way. *Carmen* evolved into one of the exotic archetypes of Western culture. It is this stereotype of Gypsy backward naïveté that Lakis Lazopoulos exploits in his satirical Greek TV show, *Al-Tsantiri News*; and it is the same imagery that inspired Dimitris Papaioannou in his spectacular opening ceremony of the Olympic Games at Athens in 2004.

What we have in all these cases is established Western stereotypes reproduced in all languages of the diffused post-mediatic spectacle: in the *Al-Tsantiri News* parody, Gypsy naïveté absolves the sayings of the narrator/protagonist, while the caricature of the watermelon peddler who plies the streets in his pickup truck, surrounded by merry Gypsy girls, becomes a symbol for the "carefree fete" that opens the Olympic Games before the eyes of billions of television viewers. Roma culture is integrated into the globalised tourism of images under the terms of the postmodern exotic gaze.

You will realise that, although challenged, these stereotypes continue to confine Roma behaviours and lifestyles within certain enclosed—and hence clear—patterns which have to do more with our own gaze. In a strange way, the verse of William Carlos Williams comes back, reversed this time: "The pure products… go crazy."

On the contrary, the Roma culture is one that exalts all kinds of recombination and do-it-yourself, the mayhem of bricolage with the use of disparate leftover objects and materials and the dexterity of the junk dealer (who preserves and recycles the memory of urban objects). But allow me to take this one step further. The Italian political thinker Paulo Virno cites, in his *Grammar of the Multitude*, four key concepts of post-Fordism: opportunism, cynicism, chatting and curiosity.[9] If we attempt to expand these concepts, we will find them, to a lesser or greater degree, in the behaviours of Roma communities. In other words, we will see their special adaptability to conditions of temporariness and vertiginous insecurity through constant repairs and mechanisms of survival.

So we find ourselves before a paradox, which centres not on how to 'intervene' into the Roma way of living and working but on how we can learn from them, how we can perceive a series of new phenomena in our society through their experiences. It may sound like an exaggeration, but this may be what one would have felt in 1972 if they came across *Learning from Las Vegas* by Robert Venturi, Denise Scott Brown and Steven Izenour. What have we learnt since then? That we can make positive use of things that at first seem disturbing and repulsive or against which we have got used to being negatively predisposed. In our case, this kind of amassed experience turns into how we can learn from these cultures of vagueness, uncertainty, flexible habitation, remix and mobility. Under the condition of post-Fordist capitalism, instead of assimilating the Roma into our ways an increasing number of social groups begin to live and work like them.

Yorgos Tzirtzilakis, is associate Professor at the University of Thessaly Greece, Department of Architecture

Dimitris Papaioannou Opening Ceremony of the Athens 2004 Olympic Games.

HISTORY MIGRATION

IS TRADITION THE ENEMY OF HISTORY?

Thomas Acton

Transcript of a paper presented at the *Gypsy Survival Strategies* seminar, London College of Fashion 22 June 2009.

Within the overall theme of Survival, I will ask whether perhaps tradition is the enemy of history, that appreciation of history can assure Survival.

We are in the middle of Gypsy, Roma, Traveller History Month and many people, many Romany intellectuals, have begun to believe quite passionately that an examination and revision of Romany history is an important precondition for any Romany liberation. I was involved 30, 40 years ago, in the beginnings of what was then called Gypsy education in England. If you can think back to the 1960s, most Gypsy children in England who lived in caravans were excluded from school, probably less than 10 per cent attended primary school, and primary schools would actively refuse them. That went on into the 1970s. Near the end of the Labour government, when Croydon specifically excluded a Traveller girl from school, in 1977, on the grounds that she didn't belong to that area, we failed to get anything out of Shirley Williams who was then the Secretary of State for Education.

It was actually Rhodes Boyson who, in 1980, as the Schools Minister in Margaret Thatcher's government, issued a circular which essentially said that all schools had the duty to take in children irrespective of the area from which they came from. That was part of Tory dogma, letting more children into popular schools, but it was specifically applied to Gypsy and Travellers. So you can say that the legal right of Gypsy and Travellers and Romany people to education in England was really only established in 1980. Wasn't it the 1944 Education Act that established a duty on parents to send their children to school? It didn't establish a duty on schools to accept their children. That battle had yet to be won.

In the 1970s and 80s, people said that Traveller children in schools wanted just reading, writing and arithmetic—something that would help them to do the books for their business, or maybe get a proper job. The last thing they… [would] be interested in was history. And of course, history as it was taught throughout most of England excluded Gypsies. You would think it was quite important that there existed a population in Britain who… [were] survivor[s] of genocide. But no, genocide was taught as something that was done by Germans. English school children aren't even taught that the British Empire enthusiastically committed genocide in Tasmania, let alone that it had a policy of genocide, for nearly a century, against Gypsies, from the middle of the sixteenth to the middle of the seventeenth century. And though in that sense history was self-burying, so that even Travellers themselves are barely aware of it, the effects linger. During my field research 30

to 40 years ago, one of the English Romany phrases, with which parents threatened their children was "you'll be *bichadi pawdle*!" What does that mean? *Bichadi*—sent, pawdle—across, short for "*bichadi pawdle the bori lon pani*". Transported. I mean, the last Gypsies were actually transported to Australia in the 1860s. But Gypsy parents on the side of the A13 of Barking were threatening their children that this might happen to them in 1967, 1968, and 1970.

Tradition implies a traditional knowledge; but seeing yourself as traditional doesn't by itself enable you to re-examine how it happened that people got to the position of transportation, and how… the fact [that] people from England were murdered, just for being Gypsies, get lost from history. That is one of the main foci of Romani Studies.

I have been working on Gypsies for 40 years, but I guarantee you, once or twice a month, when people learn that I am a professor of Romani studies they will sidle up to me and whisper in my ear, "of course, you do know that they are not all true Gypsies" as though they are in possession of some esoteric knowledge about Gypsies that I, who have been working on Gypsies for 40 years, might not have cottoned on to. I mean, if you think about it for a moment, it is absurd, yet many, many ordinary people believe that they are in possession of a great secret that not a lot of people know, that there are a lot of people that are only pretending to be Gypsies. This is one of the peculiarities of British racism about Gypsies, and to a lesser extent other countries of North Western Europe. It is rather different in Eastern Europe where there is a tendency to consider any marginalised people as Gypsies. You actually find it in that extraordinary racist United Nations development programme report in Gypsies in 2004, which did a survey of Gypsies and about 7 per cent of the respondents said that they weren't Gypsies but they were poor people living near Gypsies, and yet they were designated as Gypsies by the social workers who chose the survey sample for the researchers. So sometimes the ideology of the "true Gypsies" can be turned on its head. The complexities of racial stereotyping of Gypsies, Roma, Travellers, are enormous and I think it is fair to say that they are more complex even than those relating to Jews, who suffer from probably the next most complex bundle of stereotypes.

Now, is the secret to Gypsies' survival their tradition? Is modernity the enemy of Gypsies? Now I actually hate both concepts. As a sociologist, the reason I can't be a postmodernist is that I have never accepted the reification of modernity in the first place. It's a kind of chronological essentialism—taking a period of time and treating it as though it had a spirit of itself, which is independent of the things, which happened in that period of time. It was first satirised by Molière in his wonderful play, perhaps the first postmodernist play, *Le Malade Imaginaire*, 1673, where the quack doctor feels for somebody's heart on the right hand side and somebody says, "isn't it on the left hand side" and he says "*Nous avons changé tout çela*", "we have changed all that": the very spirit of modernity! Somebody asks him, "Why does opium send people to sleep?" and he says because opium has a *virtus dormativa*—"a sleepy spirit", literally. The great fraudulent thing is that it sounds like an explanation, but it is just a vacuous definition. To say why things are happening today is because of modernity, is tautological, that things are happening today because today is today. It is vacuous as an explanation, even in the hands of Zygmunt Bauman. I defy you to read the whole works of Zygmunt Bauman, who is someone I quite revere as a sociologist, but go through and see if you cannot just substitute "modernity", in all of his works… [for] the words "industrial society". Postmodernity is just the decomposition of industrial society. It's the opposite of a metaphor, it's an abstraction, which obscures. Modernity is not an explanation of anything: you need a real explanation. Industrialisation, urbanisation, these are explanations. But the use of the word modernity of course is a cunning ploy, to take people away from looking at where actual human interests are involved. People are trying to get what they want out of history, so when Tony Blair says, of almost anything that he wants to happen in the Labour party, that it is necessary to modernise it, modern is just an abstractifying way of saying, "what I want is…". And it's opposed to tradition, which is supposed to be conservative, what we have handed down—so people of tradition are typified as stuck in the past.

But the most important thing about Romany culture is that it has tremendous traditions of innovation and adaptation. For example, the most important Gypsy trades today are not the trades like peg making, or metal recycling, but those trades which Gaje (non-Gypsies) have not yet realised are Gypsy trades. The new trades are the Gypsy computer salesmen, the Gypsy vacuum cleaner retailer. I even discovered that the doormats in the entrances of a large building I visit regularly, are supplied by a Gypsy business. The tradesman has a website and phone line, he collects the old mats and replace them with new ones. He is from a family that has been trading carpets for generations. In fact Gypsy carpet traders are one of the archetypal Gypsy trades, going back to the Ottoman Empire and beyond. Would he be working for the corporation that owns the building if they knew he was a Gypsy? He is running the business from his laptop in his caravan and he contracted out the website design to another Gypsy and he is not going to take the risk of divulging his background. The key to survival is adaptation, for which culture gives us the tools. Surviving genocide or slavery was the biggest adaptation of all and an adaptation that damaged the survivors in many ways.

So going back to the question of history, the first thing is who are the Roma and where do they come from? I'm not going to give you an answer because in a sense all of the answers are constructed. I am going along with the social constructionists only so far, but in a sense I am going along with it pragmatically, because if I am with English Gypsies and they say "You don't want to believe all that stuff about us coming from India, my granddad said we came from Egypt, it's in the Bible and my pastor said we probably came from Egypt too, and that's what I believe", I will answer "well okay, I have met people in Yugoslavia who believe the exact same thing and that's fine", "… And we are called Romany because we roam around", "… Well that's part of the connotation of the word Romany within England."

I will challenge, but only if people want to get into a debate, only if they demand to contrast their standpoint with my own.

So what is the academic standpoint? A very basic picture was established by nineteenth century racism that Gypsies are an Indian race. This replaced the earlier narrative that Gypsies were a naughty nomadic minority in Western Europe, pretending to have come from Egypt, who dyed their skin to look darker. (The story about Roma in much of Eastern Europe was a little different.) In Western Europe, generally speaking, Gypsies were considered a deviant, begging minority in the seventeenth and early eighteenth century, an image which was replaced from the 1780s onward by the idea that they were a racial minority, and also that they were racially primitive because on their journey from India or Egypt to Europe, over the course of 500 years or so, they still hadn't assimilated into European society, [that] they still wandered around. So we could say that Gypsies formed a confirming exception in the nineteenth century to traditional racism; they were the exception that proved the rule. They were Europeans, but still racially primitive. In the twentieth century this racism was sometimes quasi-benevolent, suggesting "we" need to preserve "them" as if we would preserve a dinosaur if we found one. Tragically, this quasi-benevolent racial antiquarianism faded and was transformed into the exclusionary and ultimately murderous racism of eugenics, which says "well actually we don't need primitive people around; we only need civilised advanced people around. We need to put them into reservations and ultimately, perhaps to kill them."

Racism persisted longer in Romani studies than any other area of social science. The 1961 *Journal of the Gypsy Lore Society* published an article by Herman Arnold, (who, it was later established, had links to the Nazi bureaucracy which interned and then murdered Gypsies), which was entitled 'The Gypsy Gene'. He asserted that Gypsies had only settled when they had been hybridised by surrounding peoples. His main defender in Eastern Europe was Josef Vekerdi, a librarian in the Budapest public library who was active and influential into 1980s until he was denounced by a new generation of sociologists and largely discredited. He remained, however, very influential in the Ministry of Education in Hungary. Racism was only comprehensively challenged in the 1960s by people like Professor Ian Hancock, by myself and by Jean-Pierre Liégeois in France who presented an alternative, 'anti-racist' paradigm, or post-racism paradigm.

And insofar as there is any alternative explanative paradigm. I suppose we bring it out of a certain kind of Marxism, and to some extent, I'll whisper it, I remain Marxist. I still think that material conditions actually explain the form racism takes. Particularly, I look to the Romanian sociologist PN Panaitescu, whose 1941 essay in the *Journal of the Gypsy Lore Society* provides a Marxist account of slavery in Romania, which could be considered the basis of an alternative approach to Romany history. It treats culture as something that has to be explained.

Genocide is something that has to be explained; culture doesn't explain genocide, genocide explains culture. Change in culture occurs because of technological change and consequent shifts in class position. In particular, I have argued [that] the development of agricultural capitalism in the sixteenth century led to genocide in Western Europe and slavery within Romanian neo-feudalism. Panaitescu's piece is a very pregnant little essay; arguably he does for Romani studies what WEB Dubois did for Black Studies. The other great Romanian Marxist is Henri Stahl who sets Roma in the context of his study of traditional Romanian villages. It is rather sad to see that many contemporary Romanian writers don't give Panaitescu and Stahl due credit, or understand the extent to which they provide a means of unmasking and constructing the contours of Romanian racism.

Instead, sadly one can still hear a Romanian social commentator saying that the legacy of centuries of slavery can not easily be overcome, so Romanian racism is understandable!

This Marxist alternative to racism did not, however, really catch on (least of all in "Communist" Romania). Instead we find developing an a-theoretical non-racist approach, rejecting racism as non-natural—and therefore almost inexplicable. Angus Fraser, who wrote the 1991 history *The Gypsies*, explicitly abandoned racism as a general explanatory schema in the 1960s but this left a void in his thought; in his later work he does not attempt general explanations and is sceptical of them in others. He starts off in the 1950s using racist explanations, but he saw the light in the 1960s in his critique of Gypsylorists like Brian Vesey-Fitzgerald and Dora Yates (alongside Augustus John who, in his preface to one of Dominic Reeves' books said that "the ideology of the 'True Gypsy' was just racial nonsense").

So Angus Fraser abandoned racism as a general explanatory schema but didn't put anything in its place, which left him open to the challenge by the revisionists, like Willems and Lucassen who asserted [that] "Gypsies did not necessarily come from India, and could have made up their language." The English Gypsy social constructionist Brian Belton follows their position that the modern Gypsy identity was more or less invented by Grellmann in 1783. He has recently developed and moderated this social constructionist position. Nonetheless, the social constructionist position still cannot respond to the challenge from the linguists that the Romani language can only be accounted for by a migration from India of at least some of the Gypsies' ancestors.

This brute fact, however, does not serve to make sense of Romani history by itself. Migrations are not explicable by the fact that some Gypsies in contemporary Europe are commercial nomads, as though they could have just wandered all the way from India, because commercial nomads need a protector, they have to have the right social conditions for doing it. Equally, the simple-minded Romani nationalist position, that Roma were a military caste that came to Europe is equally implausible; such social formations don't just maraud as military adventurers for the sake of it.

Those academics that are themselves of Romany heritage will require a sociologically plausible account of the origin of the Gypsies, and the modified historical revisionism thesis offered by Professor Hancock and Dr Adrian Marsh is a first stab at this. It suggests that the social construction story is to some extent true, except that it didn't happen in Germany in the 1780s; it actually took place in Turkey in the late eleventh or early twelfth century. They suggest that the Dom and the Rom developed similar historical political-military identities—the Dom in the eighth century, and the Rom in the eleventh century—as multi-caste medieval Hindu armies. They suggest the Roma, or more precisely the Romany language, may have started as the command language of a Hindu militia in the Muslim Ghaznavid army. This language was not necessarily the native tongue of all the fighters, because Medieval armies were diverse societies on the move (Medieval Indian armies were multi-caste and multi-cultural), but all the members of such an army had to speak the language of its commanders. The Dom has a similar history, only two or three centuries earlier. These were very diverse military formations. Hancock and Marsh suggest that Roma only gels as an ethnic identity after their defeat in Anatolia. Maybe this proto-Romany army enjoyed quasi-autonomy up until the twelfth century, when, after the Ghaznavids were defeated, they fought alongside the Armenians against the Seldjuks and the Ottomans. The last Armenian principality was defeated only in 1361 and only after that do we get unambiguous accounts of people who can only have been Roma in Western Europe.

These 'late origin' theories of Romany are inspiring new PhD studies about Roma, but the revision of history is not just an academic phenomenon, it's a popular phenomenon across the world. Here in Britain there is the Romany and Traveller Family History Society with over 600 members mostly of

Romany origin who have realised that they can't understand their family's history without understanding the general context. This implies that we need to look at the differences between Western European Gypsies, between those in Northern Europe, in Spain, in the Ottoman border regions of Romania and Serbia, and the Balkans. Each one of these has different and differencing reactions to the catastrophe that the foundation of the nation-state was for Romany people in the sixteenth century. The nation-state was founded in genocide and ethnic cleansing, and we have seen [that] they are the condition[s] of its perpetuation. The nation-state, however, began to decompose, or at least its boundaries became permeable, in the early eighteenth century, which led to the collapse of (feudal) slavery and migration from Eastern Europe. The layering of the Romany communities in the rest of the world occurred as successive migrant communities arrived, and even more recently in the UK during the accession of new countries to the European Union. So we have two sets of people who call themselves Roma in the West: those who came here before 1914, and the recent Roma arrivals since 1989.

The coalition building between the different populations of Roma, Gypsies and Travellers cannot be done without deconstructing the history which connects them. Unless we learn the lessons of past oppressions we will suffer new ones. Our understanding of Roma is linked to their history; we cannot deal with the history of slavery and genocide unless we deconstruct the racist accounts of it. Uncritical tradition is no substitute for critical history. History is the key and that is why this Gypsy, Roma, Traveller History Month is so important.

Thomas Acton is Professor of Romani Studies, University of Greenwich, UK.

PREVIOUS PAGE
Kalderash children from the Campo Boario in Rome, outside their mobile home.

BELOW
LAN workshop with the Kalderasha in Rome, Italy.

TEATRO INDIA
ROME ITALY

The former Miralanza factory was squatted by Romanian families. Abandoned industrial buildings are suitable for seasonal immigrants who build lightweight shelters using recycled materials. Neighbours rejected their presence and the Teatro India settlement was set on fire. Fortunately there were no casualties.

TOP
Aerial view of former
Miralanza factory.

BOTTOM
These young boys told EU Roma
that they are working for a living
and never steal. They migrated from
a sedentary rural community in
Romania several months ago.

OPPOSITE TOP
Shelters are built from
recycled materials.

OPPOSITE BOTTOM
Tents are used for transitory living,
especially for migrating communities.

View of the Miralanza factory after
the fire on 3 January 2008.

KALDERASHA
ROME ITALY

Karen Bermann and Alex Valentino

The Kalderasha of Rome is a very distinct Roma cultural group. They are Italian citizens of Hungarian decent over several generations. In Italian, Zingaro (Gypsy) is considered offensive, the correct denomination Kalderasha is derived from the Romanian word "*caldarar*", meaning "cauldron maker". The via Santa Maria dei Caldarari in the Jewish ghetto of Rome references the place where they and other metalworkers once practiced their trade. Indeed, this group, like Kalderasha in general around Europe, continues the tradition of artisanal metalworking.

The populations of the Kalderasha settlements in Rome vary from 80 to 200 people. This flux is due to their forced nomadic way of life, a term which describes the difficulty that they, and almost all Roma, have of finding a legal or permanent location to settle in. Throughout our studies we have found that Roma across Europe wish to live in conventional housing and nomadism has not been a cultural imperative or value for several hundreds years. A combination of poverty, discrimination, and lack of legal documents usually precludes this and forces the Roma into legal or illegal campsites or '*campo*'. The Kalderasha are generally not living in poverty and they have rights of citizenship, but they differ from other Roma cultural groups as many practice some form of nomadic behaviour and believe it is an essential aspect of Kalderasha cultural identity. The community we met refuse to live in a legal camp and have no intention of living in houses; they have large and well-equipped camper vans from which awnings, tents, kitchens, laundries, play spaces, and so on, unfurl rather magically to create an orderly and comfortable living area, partly indoor, partly outdoor.

The Italian government does not recognise the legitimacy of this nomadic way of life, and so the Kalderasha campers are subject to the same rules and penalties as any vehicle parked too long on one spot. The city authorities have not cooperated with their requests for "*diritto di sosta*", a place to stop and reside with their families. Cultural difference is clearly an issue; a mobile home—and even more a community of moving houses—is an alien concept within mainstream European social culture.

During the EU-Roma survey, the Kalderasha group splintered and reformed after several evictions. Mapping in this case came to mean a report on the recent history of the group's forced

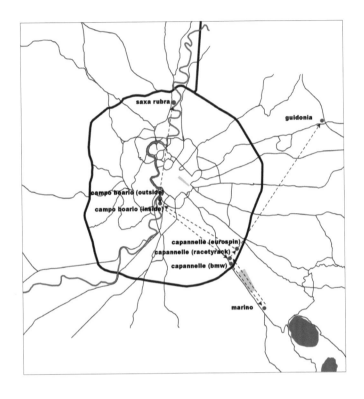

TOP
Map of the displacement and splintering of the Kalderasha community from the Campo Boario settlement to other districts of Rome.

BOTTOM
Time line of occupation and eviction of the Campo Boario.

OPPOSITE TOP
Kalderasha in Palermo, Italy 1966. Photographic archive of Aldo Udorovic.

OPPOSITE CENTRE
Kalderasha in Naples, Italy 1966. Photographic archive of Aldo Udorovic.

1992-2007: Campo Boario (permanent)

1986-2007: Campo Boario (seasonal)

| 1991 | 1992 | 1993 | 1994 | 1995 | 1996 | 1997 | 1998 |

1	Testa
2	Saxa
3	Capa
4	Palag
5	Capa
6	Capa
7	Testa
8	Guido

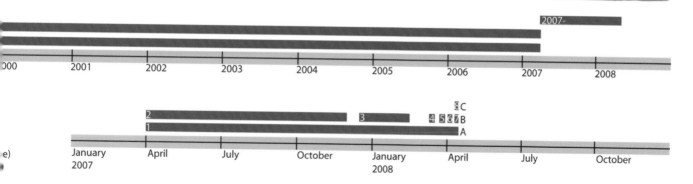

nomadic status, their relationship with the city government, the media's presentation of their situation, and their movements in and around the city. EU-Roma documented the ways in which they continued to practice their craft under these unstable and peripatetic conditions. It also became evident that the right to a place to live cannot be separated from cultural, civil, and human rights.

ON THE MOVE

In 1986, after years of moving from place to place, from Tor Bella Monaca to Borgata Romania, the Kalderasha of Rome began looking for a more permanent location and came across the neighbourhood of Testaccio at the ex-Mattatoio. Within the rundown walls of this abandoned slaughterhouse complex there existed a cluster of aging buildings and a neglected expanse of paving. The complex, which was built toward the end of the nineteenth century adjacent to the Tiber River, had been left to decay since it closed in 1970. A mixed group took up residency: artists, community activists, a social centre, drug users, and weeds. Carriage drivers also kept their horses in stables here, a longstanding tradition. The group peacefully moved into the Campo Boario section of the ex-Mattatoio, and with the quiet cooperation of the Comune di Roma, inhabited the nine acre lot, arranging their campers and caravans in what would be their semi-permanent home for several years. Due to the security, urban centrality, and economical benefit of the location, the Kalderasha began to establish a more permanent residency in early 1990.

While sharing this location with stables for horse-drawn carriage drivers, as well as a small group of Kurdish people who arrived in 1999, they carried on their daily lives, raising their families and staying actively involved in their traditional craft of metalworking. According to Aldo Udorovich, a member of and spokesperson for the Kalderasha group, a number of their children attended nearby schools in Testaccio, and the group as a whole had friendly relationships with the surrounding community.

BELOW

Campo Boario settlement inside the former slaughter house—Mattatoio in the Testaccio district of Rome.

OPPOSITE

Kalderasha elders, Yanco and Aldo relaxing outside their caravans.

In 2004, the group established a formal agreement with the city of Rome allowing them the right to stay at Campo Boario. This agreement turned out to be non-binding, as city officials arrived at the ex-Mattatoio in late 2006 ordering an eviction so they could begin the development of a new project, Cittá dell'Altra Economia (City of the Other Economy), a fair trade market aimed at regenerating the surrounding community. The Kalderasha fought back and requested that the city buy or provide new land for them; the city refused, offering only to temporarily rent land to them. After further requests from the Kalderasha for assistance in finding an alternative location, even if temporary, and damages for their troubles, the city came back with an offer. It proposed to give a sum of 2,000 Euro per family, but continued to decline to provide assistance for alternative living arrangements. The community asked the city to use the money to buy them a plot of land for semi-permanent use; the city declined. Aldo Udorovich characterises the tone of the officials' responses with whom he met: "It's okay, you are used to moving!" This refers not only to this group's history of forced movement before their years at Campo Boario but also suggests a very common misunderstanding of Roma culture.

Realising that the city was not going to redress their losses, the group set off in their camper vans in search of a new home. They always sought to stop legally, with the permission of the municipality or, in the case of private land, of the owner. But they were not always successful in finding such a space and often stopped in out-of-the way empty areas in order to avoid conflict and confrontation. In the past year and a half, the Kalderasha group, formerly of Campo Boario, have split into smaller groups, as the viable sites around the city do not have enough space to accommodate their entire community. One group, intent on keeping their children in the Testaccio schools, moved just outside the walls of the ex-Mattatoio, on a dead-end street along the Tiber River, and set up camp there. Another group moved north to the small community of Saxa Rubra and for ten months joined a pre-existing group of their relatives who had been living in this location since the 1990s. The entire group was evicted in January 2008, forcing their move to the parking lot of a BMW dealer in the area of Capannelle, then to the town of Marino, then just outside the Capannelle horsetrack, and then to a Lidl parking lot in Capannelle. A few hours after their arrival in the parking lot they were visited by a number of military and city police, aggressively requesting that they leave the area due to complaints from neighbours, even though they had permission from the president of the local municipality and from the Commune to stay for five days. The president of the municipality arrived on the scene and confirmed that he had indeed agreed to this arrangement, at which point the police departed. Unexpected visits from the police lasting several hours were not unusual occurrences.

At lunchtime on the fifth day, over 100 local residents appeared in the parking lot to advise the Kalderasha that it was time to leave. Seven campervans moved back to the Lungotevere in Testaccio to join the group that had been living there since the eviction from the Campo Boario. The rest went outside the city to a small community called Guidonia.

EU-Roma met the group in April 2008 just hours before they left the horse track at Capannelle and followed them to the supermarket parking lot. We observed the encounter with police, during which we were forbidden to take photos, a video camera was confiscated and the footage deleted by a police officer. Two members of our group also had their passports confiscated by the police while they made a variety of phone calls, ostensibly checking on the legality of the documents. During the process of mapping the events, we subsequently followed the group that remained in the city and joined others already encamped outside the walls of the Mattatoio, doing our best to keep a record of the forced nomadism and until an agreement is made with the city or a private landowner, the continuous movement of the past 18 months looks like their only future.

Karen Bermann is a Professor of Architecture Iowa State University, USA.

OPPOSITE TOP AND BOTTOM

Final police eviction of the
Campo Boario Kalderasha
on 6 June 2008.

RIGHT
Kalderasha kitchen extension.

BOTTOM
Laundry area in the parking lot
of the Capannelle district Rome.

OPPOSITE
Kalderasha women in their caravan.

OPPOSITE

This ghetto on Baneasa Street consists of 22 prefabricated containers 2.4 x 6 metres. The average number of persons living in one container is just over five. There is only one source of water for the entire community of 120 people.

BELOW

The former administrative building of a local pig farm is home to around 20 families. There are apartments situated in the basement, with no ventilation or natural light. On the facade is a plaque stating that the facility has been refurbished and is administered by the Romanian government through the National Agency for the Roma.

OVERLEAF

The Roma community was promised they would move back into the block of flats after refurbishment, but four years has gone by. They are urban dwellers and former industrial workers but since the regime changed in Romania they obtain only temporary jobs. Some began retrofitting the containers to extend the living space and they attempted to drain the damp soil, a former wet area.

BANEASA TÎRGU MURES ROMANIA

Baneasa is situated in a former industrial area with poor transport networks to the rest of the city. It is the most recent Roma re-housing project in Romania. The community used to live in a dilapidated block of social flats on Rovinari Street. When the refurbishment began, they were evicted and formed three separate pockets of poverty and ethnic exclusion: one near the refurbished block and two official ghettos in Baneasa Street.

MAPPING THE TRAVELLER LONDON UK

Take notice, that England is not a Free People,
till the Poor that have no land, have a free
allowance to dig and labour the Commons,
and so live as Comfortably as the Landlords
that live in their Inclosures.

Gerrard Winstanley[1]

We are the last links with independence and
self sufficiency in an over organised country.
Shuffling along our own courses, we elude to a
great extent the tentacles of officialdom which
seek to enclose everyone within their grasp,
plotting their lives by standards, times and dates.
Freedom we are told is everyman's heritage-yet
how few achieve it and how few exploit it.

Dominic Reeve[2]

The two statements above, written several hundred years apart,
both describe a disparity between conceptual expectations
of a right to 'freedom' in a democratic society, and the actual
manifestation of this in our daily lives.

Embarking on the EU-Roma study of Roma housing in London,
from a background perspective of affordable housing design, we
swiftly found ourselves embedded in technicalities. Ethnic and
legal definitions of 'Gypsy' and 'Traveller' appear to be fluid in the
UK, and frequently involve perceived connections just as much as
literal ones. Throughout England one can call oneself a 'traveller'
without any ethnic inheritance, just as one can be ethnically Roma
and conduct a sedentary existence in standardised Housing
Association accommodation. In contrast to the research of other
EU-Roma partners, there are no clearly delineated Roma groups
occupying the edge-lands of London. In essence, we found
ourselves simultaneously investigating the idea of a London
'traveller' in conjunction with the everyday reality of a Gypsy,
Roma, Traveller existence. We found ourselves not learning about
these people, but learning from them—and the potent ideas their
history reveals about wider society in London and the UK.

Through a chain of events, which is still the subject of rigorous
academic debate as Professor Hancock so rightly states, mobility
and nomadism lie at the heart of Roma history. The difference
between 'traveller' existence and conventional society is a source
of both conflict and romance. For time immemorial, people have
longed for the 'freedom' embodied in the idea of a nomadic
existence, whilst simultaneously we have feared it, demonised it,
and legislated against it. It symbolises a breakdown in the order
of governance as we know it and the potential for radical chaos.

But, the more marginalised the notion becomes, perhaps, the
more we long for it. If we look back into history, the 'traveller'
existence was not always so distinct from the rest of society.
Common land is the thread that ties the two together prior to the
sweeping changes brought about by the legislative acts of the
seventeenth century. With much of the country considered to
be 'in common' prior to this, it was far easier to forage an existence
off the land, whilst remaining relatively untroubled by concerns
about land ownership. With the advent of 'parliamentary
enclosure' in the seventeenth and eighteenth centuries, so
despised by Gerrard Winstanley, huge swathes of the country
suddenly became off limits, stifling the individuals capacity to
move and settle freely and limiting the use of such land for the
poor for grazing animals, gathering food and fuel. Such acts
damaged the viability of a nomadic or semi-nomadic existence,
but they also worsened circumstances for the rural poor.

There was still evidence of non-Gypsy people working on an
itinerant basis in the nineteenth and early twentieth centuries,
and the value of a mobile workforce seems to have been well
understood. To take a particular example, the Gypsy occupation
of horse trading, wherein a travelling population served settled
farms and businesses by selling them new horses, relied upon a
mobile existence. Genetically, the introduction of new animals from
elsewhere was an efficient means by which to improve the stock of
one's own stable. Associated smithy skills were also valuable. So,
whilst there is plenty of evidence of the settled population fearing
the 'otherness' of Gypsy groups, a mutual interdependence
existed which continued to make a roadside existence viable. In
London terms, such interdependence can be seen in the seasonal
shifts of the economic city: 'Gypsy' camps existed on the edges of
the city (often on parcels of leftover common land). Street names
such as Gipsy Hill and Romany Road in Lambeth, as commonly
found in many London suburbs, remain to bear testament to the
influence of travelling communities on the city. Whilst maintaining
a traveller existence, many Gypsies owned permanent yards in the
East End, thereby positioning themselves to utilise the benefits
of an itinerant existence with the economies of the city's street
markets. In September, working class Londoners would leave the
city en-masse in search of work hop-picking in Kent; away from
their normal existence they would 'hop' in tandem with Gypsy
communities: in effect, seasonal relocation for economic reasons
was shared by settled and nomadic people. Lifestyles interwove.

With the passing of the 'Caravan Sites Act' of 1968, coinciding
with a peak in caravan holidaying, the viability of a roadside existence
was again dramatically reduced, with the UK government openly
hoping that Gypsies and other travelling people would become
completely integrated among the settled population. It obliged local
authorities to provide sites for travellers—which few initially did—and
also brought in new laws to reduce the capacity for a traveller to
set up a temporary home on marginal land. Sites, which had been
used by travellers for decades, if not centuries, were adopted by
local authorities, a significant example being Thistlebrook Way in the
London Borough of Greenwich. Such sites have become normalised
in subsequent decades, and now benefit from the provision of
utility services and postcodes, inevitably reducing the occupant's
relationship to a 'traveller' existence. No longer the informal and
autonomous camps they once were, nevertheless, in many cases,
they have become strong communities in their own right—and in so
doing a new form of 'traveller' lifestyle has emerged.

TOP

Thistlebrook, Manner Way in the London Borough of Greenwich, SE2 contains 38 pitches of mobile and prefabricated homes. The community is a mixture of English Romany Gypsies and non-Romany.

BOTTOM

Eleanor Street in the London Borough of Tower Hamlets, E3 has 19 pitches, mainly Irish Travellers in both mobile and permanent homes.

TOP
Cohabitation of prefabricated house with caravan in Thistlebrook, Manner Way.

BOTTOM
Parkway Crescent, situated in London E15 is a gated community of Romany Gypsy and Irish Traveller homes, which moved from the Clays Lane 2012 Olympic Park development. It contains a combination of 13 pitches with both mobile and permanent dwellings.

OVERLEAF
EU-Roma Mapping—Roma, Gypsy and Traveller communities across London, 2009.

The 'Gypsy'—as a human being and as an idea, has held a significant and captivating presence in UK society for hundreds of years; whether in the realms of literature, art, music, film or fashion. It is poignant that, as the last vestiges of Gypsy 'wagon-time' were removed from UK culture, much debate in art and architecture was focussed on ideals of nomadism. Whether the politically charged *homo ludens* developed by Guy Debord and the Situationists, the urban nomad at the scale of human or city of Archigram, or the utilitarian social mobility of Cedric Price, the avant-garde of architectural thought began to investigate the nomadic lifestyle just as it lost its viability as an everyday existence. As architects, we were educated in this tradition, and the potency of these nomadic visions remain.

Every week, we see prototypical 'nomadic' or 'mobile' structures in the pages of the architectural press—'interventions', romantic gestures, new ways of reading, or interrogating an environment. This sits alongside a simultaneous rise of a new wave of low impact 'place in the country' structures for those who can afford them. Such structures hint at ideas of lightness, mobility, transience and freedom which remain out of reach, and in the words of Superstudio: "Architecture remains at the edge of our life, and intervenes only at certain points in the process, usually when behaviour has already been codified, furnishing answers to rigidly stated problems."

Architects dream of nomadism, but build permanence. While as a larger society we cling to mortgaged homes, we indulge ourselves in holidays in tents, 'mobile homes' and narrow boats. 'traveller' existence, in this sense, has become a tamed glimpse of living with the elements. The standard 'mobile home' possesses a towing bracket and miniature wheels rarely sufficient for serviceable towing.

Today, we are accustomed to our rights being entrenched in provable identity, itself closely connected to an address and place of abode, whilst the economics on which we rely grow ever further from our everyday existence and from tangibility. The Londoner can be tracked with ease by credit card transactions and public transport payment systems like the Oyster card. GPS technology, in the mobile phones in our pockets, has become an invaluable navigational aid whilst also having the capacity to describe our movements and lifestyles—a phenomenon investigated by the artist Jeremy Wood in his GPS Drawings. Even our bodies are logged and catalogued.

These processes are the subject of much debate, with some sections of society seeing them as fundamentally altering human rights, and others following the adage that "if you don't do anything wrong, you don't have anything to hide". "Wrong", of course, is a flexible concept, a cultural artefact, and indeed the traveller existence neatly fits into a normalised contemporary sense of wrong.

An example of this is the difficulty with which a travelling community disposes of its rubbish—illegal dumping is definitively 'wrong' in the context of a society which analyses its neighbour's recycling bins for signs of overindulgence. In contemporary Britain, 'traveller' life styles prevent conventional participation, contribution and accountability whilst operating outside of what Dominic Reeve terms, "the tentacles of officialdom".

The association of rights with address and identity is evidenced in the lifestyles of recent Roma refugees in the UK. The London Boroughs' Traveller Needs Assessment of March 2008 suggests that today's Roma populations in the UK are eager to live in 'normal' dwellings, and as a result many are currently settled in government-subsided Housing Association homes, making it easier to apply for jobs and gain access to essential rights and services. As an unsurprising consequence of a history of detrimental legislation, most 'traveller' populations, of any ethnicity, have become sedentary. The Assessment document also indicates that while only a small percentage of London's 13,500 'travellers' still desire a 'life on the road', many miss the intense relations with other people made possible by the caravan and similar forms of dwelling. Meanwhile, effort is being made towards generating a 'Gypsy, Roma, Traveller' communal sense of identity through identifying shared aspects of heritage and contemporary existence, however it manifests itself. Such a sense of identity is well portrayed in the annual UK Gypsy Roma Traveller History Month in 2008 and 2009.

In neighbourhood regeneration, much effort is expended on allowing for diversity. Bodies of knowledge such as the 1993 document "Accommodating Diversity" aim to ensure that we are designing homes that are aware of the needs of different ethnic groups—without particularly shifting the idea of what these homes should look like and how they should be built. Having evolved a normalised template for life, we are now expanding it to accommodate a diverse demographic, and this process is carried across into the design of traveller sites, themselves now the subject of design guidance. However, the established Victorian-based model of the home is arguably already an outmoded starting point. A broader spectrum of living arrangements are frequently called for to more effectively accommodate twenty first century lifestyles, values and living choices. Whilst we hope to house and celebrate the diversity of people, we are simultaneously witnessing the power of people to affect their homes and living environments being reduced. It is worth mentioning that the heritage of travelling peoples is usually well evidenced in whatever dwellings they now find themselves in.

No longer obliged to provide 'traveller' sites, local authorities are, perhaps inadvertently, codifying ad-hoc community structures into a settled typography. These add some more normalised attributes to the service buildings and caravans—such as boundary fences, but otherwise maintain close internal relationships between dwellers and maintain interpersonal links which appear to be much more valued—a possible legacy of 'wagon-time'. Such designs could be seen to mediate between a traveller-originated typology and an urban form that is more acceptable to the average settled community. This process has had profound social effects: when the Clays Lane traveller site in Newham was moved as a result of the 2012 Olympics, residents protested at being moved, worrying about existing social structures, access to jobs and their children's education. In an economy where a traveller existence is almost unworkable, people adapt to an existence based upon settlement. Travellers are also developing their own long-term sites leading to tension in communities as 'settled' people rarely consider a 'traveller site', no matter how well kept or how permanent, to be a good neighbour. The fear of 'otherness' is still in place. Until the systems and policy's that define our built environment are sufficiently relaxed to enable and facilitate the maximisation of individual and community enterprise rather than restrain it, it will remain a challenge to fully achieve and embrace the real diversity that creates richness, value and distinction.

Case study by Project 35 Architects.

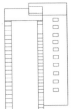

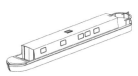

CL	City of London
B&D	London Borough of Barking and Dagenham
Ba	London Borough of Barnet
Be	London Borough of Bexley
Br	London Borough of Brent
Bro	London Borough of Bromley
Ca	London Borough of Camden
Cr	London Borough of Croydon
Ea	London Borough of Ealing
En	London Borough of Enfield
Gr	London Borough of Greenwich
Hac	London Borough of Hackney
H&F	London Borough of Hammersmith & Fulham
Hg	London Borough of Haringey
Hr	London Borough of Harrow
Hv	London Borough of Havering
Hi	London Borough of Hillingdon
Ho	London Borough of Hounslow
Is	London Borough of Islington
K&C	Royal Borough of Kensington & Chelsea
K	Royal Borough of Kingston upon Thames
La	London Borough of Lambeth
Le	London Borough of Lewisham
M	London borough of Merton
N	London Borough of Newham
Re	London Borough of Redbridge
Ri	London Borough of Richmond upon Thames
So	London Borough of Southwark
Su	London Borough of Sutton
TH	London Borough of Tower Hamlets
WF	London Borough of Waltham Forest
Wa	London Borough of Wandsworth
CW	City of Westminster

Map indicates location and relative scale of local authority traveller sites.
Dark orange circles represent proportional occupation of each site.
Pale orange circles represent proportional capacity of each site.

DIVERSITY AND TRENDS IN DWELLING
Graphics are for illustrative purposes only.

ROMA

A large proportion of Roma in London do not lead a nomadic lifestyle or live in local authority traveller sites. Research by Fordhams in 2008 suggests that Roma predominantly live in affordable housing provided by housing associations.

Research suggests that Roma are content, in general, living in 'standard' housing types. The most frequent criticism occurs when these types restrict feelings of community and engender isolation.

IRISH/ROMANY

The nature of UK law makes it difficult for those with a heritage of nomadic existence to continue this- hence the largely permanent traveller sites still provided by London, and other, local authorities.

These, and privately owned sites, are not nomadic as such but retain a strong sense of communal identity.

There is a distinct trend among these groups to move toward a settled lifestyle- particularly as it assists with plugging into local education and healthcare provision.

NEW TRAVELLERS

London and the UK has a strong culture of people who live a nomadic or semi-nomadic lifestyle out of explicit choice rather than inheritance. This includes people travelling the roads, in unoffical sites, and those on narrowboats.

There is no evidence that these groups are moving toward a settled lifestyle.

TRAVELLING SHOWPEOPLE

London and the UK retain an on-going community of travellers taking funfairs and circuses from place to place. These, with the 'new' travellers, are the group most actively engaging in a continued nomadic lifestyle, wherein their lifestyle and income-generation are firmly tied to moving on.

KEY

■ dwelling

▨ service/communal building

LB NEWHAM: CLAYS LANE CLOSE

1988-2007
13 permanent pitches
informal site layout with permanent service buildings &
mix of caravans and 'permanent' homes.
recently relocated to adjacent council-owned park for 2012 Olympics

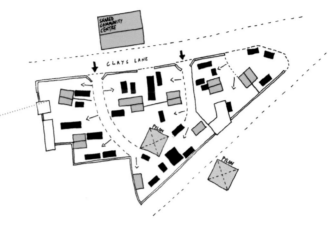

LB TOWER HAMLETS: ELEANOR STREET

19 permanent pitches
informal site layout with permanent service buildings &
mix of caravans and 'permanent' homes
backland site enclosed in all directions by rail infrastructure and
industrial buildings. proposed site of crossrail shaft indicated.
site proposed to expand into adjacent industrial areas as a result.

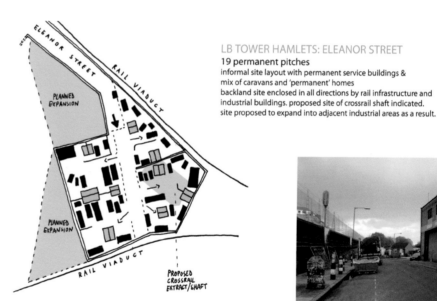

LB GREENWICH: THISTLEBROOK

40 permanent pitches
formal site layout with permanent service buildings &
mix of caravans and 'permanent' homes.
backland site surrounded by industrial buildings, Thamesmead
residential area and open ground.
traveller site predates the New Town of Thamesmead.

'It started with groups of people throwing things at or into our home. They would throw stones and also letters wrapped around these stones. The letters said that we should leave, and that gypsies should go to the gas chambers etc. They wanted us to leave Poland for the sake of racial purity.'

'Often the Romany children just sat drawing pictures whilst the other children were taught proper lessons. The teachers were of the view that Romany children could not learn and were not as bright as the Polish children.'

Asylum statements of Polish Roma, c. 2000

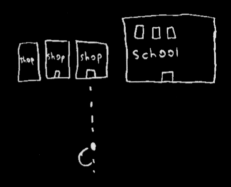

To Samanta racism is constantly being pushed to the back of the queue.

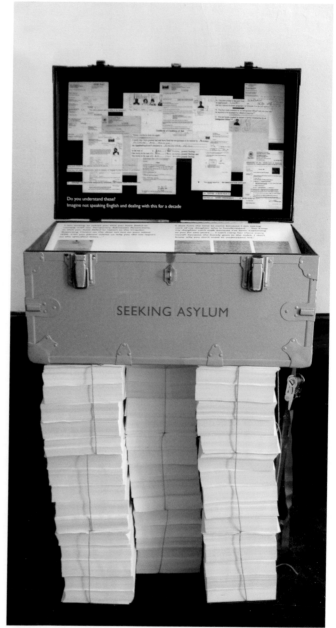

An exhibition created by EU-Roma for the Gypsy Roma Traveller History Month, June 2008.
The partners worked closely with the Roma Support Group in Newham to develop and deliver the project documenting the recent history of Polish Roma in the UK through the themes of Arrival, Seeking Asylum, EU accession and Integration and Contribution. The Roma Support Group is an association, formed in 1998 by Roma people and still led by them today, which aims to improve the quality of life of Roma refugees and migrants.

COMMUNITIES IN URBAN FRONTIERS
ISTANBUL

Aslı Kıyak İngin and Pelin Tan

Cities are in transition. Minorities or communities have a specific identity that has ethnic, religious and economical roots. This could be defined as a situated identity, which combines the relationship to and the co-existence of urban space. Over the last few years, the inhabitants and the local municipality of specific neighbourhoods of Istanbul are in a process of debate and conflict. Sulukule, the focus of this case study, is just one example. A highly Roma populated neighbourhood, made up of many districts, which are economically disadvantaged and ethnically marked, Sulukule is undergoing the process of 'urban transformation'. Urban transformation does not mean upgrading the physical environment and social condition of a rundown district, but instead, replacing the habitants and conducting projects that are valuable for urban re-development in monetary terms. Since 2006, some districts and neighbourhoods have united for solidarity, to defend their rights of dwelling. With the collaboration of academicians, independent researchers, artists and others, the neighbourhood associations are creating counter-cultural urban spaces that are not only representing the right to dwell, but also reconstructing their social-collective everyday life.

The main actors of the urban transformation projects in Turkey are KIPTAS and TOKI (Housing Development Administration of Turkey).[1] TOKI is a state department aimed at building social housing for low-income citizens. However, it is both a collaborator with municipalities and a private business responsible for urban clearance projects, which intend to replace poor, ethnically marked communities. The greater municipality of Istanbul initiated KIPTAS, to build and sell houses through a mortgage facility.[2] Working together they represent a localised version of neo-liberal urban condition and rescaling, a version of what David Harvey describes as neo-liberalism that: "... *generates a complex reconstitution of state-economy relation in which state institutions are actively mobilised to promote market-based regulatory arrangements*".[3] By introducing urban policies that allow displacement of inhabitants, shifting their ownership and property rights, using Istanbul's image as a marketing tool for local and foreign investors and manipulating urban fears (terrorism, earthquake, safety) combined, are all components that define urban clearance and rescaling. Throughout the year 2000, Istanbul witnessed the emergence of large-scale urban transformation projects under the headings of "urban renovation/urban development" which legitimised 'demolishment' and 'reconstruction' via abstract discourses of urban fear, ecology, cultural heritage and natural disasters. In 2005, the Urban Transformation and Renewal policy of 5366 accelerated the urban renovation/developments and it gave power to the municipalities to declare any district as an urban

Demolition of the building which
served as a venue for Sulukule
children's workshops on 27th
January 2009 at 7:30am.

transformation area and to control what property rights, urban planning and architectural projects could be applied.[4]

SULUKULE *MAHALLE*

Sulukule (Hatice Sultan and Neslisah Sultan neighbourhoods) is located in the historic peninsula of Istanbul, adjacent to the city's land walls—which are included in the UNESCO's World Heritage list. The whole neighbourhood falls within the City Wall Preservation Zone. The area has been able to maintain its traditional neighbourhood character and is predominantly inhabited by the Roma community. Some houses have title deeds dating from the Ottoman era. It has a remarkable cultural and demographic continuity, which is extremely rare in other parts of Istanbul. It is a neighbourhood where both tangible and intangible elements of cultural heritage co-exist and intermingle as in UNESCO's definitions of cultural heritage. The area has long been a unique centre for entertainment in Istanbul. Sulukule was severely damaged during the Vatan Street demolitions in the late 1950s; this was followed by the demolitions of 1982 and the abolition of the entertainment houses in 1992 after which the area has been condemned to urban decay.

With the enactment of law 5366 titled 'Preservation of Dilapidated Historical Buildings through Renewal and Their Sustainable Usage', the areas that were first defined as zones of "urban decay" and then declared as urban renewal zones were the historic neighbourhoods like Sulukule, Tarlabası and Süleymaniye. These projects created autonomous zones within the city and were implemented without any concern for ensuring the participation of local residents and solving their problems locally, and low-income residents were even evicted from their homes. Sulukule, which was declared a "renewal area" by a

decree issued by the Council of Ministers in 2006, and many similar areas that fall within a preservation zone, were brought under the purview of "areas that have deteriorated and lost their character", and their re-development was put on the agenda. The process of gentrification started with municipality-produced projects on the basis of the alleged adaptation of these regions to the city. The Sulukule renewal project initiated by the Municipality of Fatih proposed the entire destruction and then re-construction of 90 per cent of the region. This approach not only ignores the region's social, economic and spatial existence over centuries but also excludes residents' participation and say, thereby creating uncertainty in the region.

The majority of the homeowners opted to sell their houses to real estate speculators. According to the approved municipal renewal project, the tenants were not given the option of remaining in the neighbourhood and were offered houses in TOKI's development 48 kilometres away in Tasoluk, with 15 year mortgage instalments. Since the residents have low and irregular incomes it is almost impossible for them to commit to this payment scheme. As many of them could not adapt to their new homes and could not pay the monthly instalments, as well as heat and maintenance fees, they moved back to either Sulukule or neighbouring areas such as Karagümrük and Edirnekapı. The renewal process as a whole has caused the disintegration of the community by dispersing the existing social fabric, their inability to continue their cultural activities, their severance from social networks of solidarity, and even graver livelihood problems.

Beyond being poor, Sulukule is a neighbourhood which has a unique social, spatial, economic and cultural structure, and where these could be observed in an integrated way. It is one of the very few places which have been able to preserve this trait. In Sulukule the place where one carries on his/her existence is not home but the neighbourhood. Almost all activities,

except sleeping and cooking, are done on the narrow streets of the neighbourhood. While men spend most of their time in the neighbourhood coffeehouse, women and children have the opportunity to socialise on the streets in front of their houses. Everyone is related and born in the neighbourhood. Streets are not just spaces of circulation; they are spaces of interaction and communication where the community lives, lively spaces of association. The courtyards, unique to the area, are semi-private appendages to these streets and houses with a peculiar spatial typology that is very rarely found in Istanbul today. The street gives access to the courtyard and garden and houses are accessed through this dynamic—here as many as four or five families live. "Courtyards are communal spaces where flowerbeds and WCs are shared, laundry is washed and hung together and children play. They are usually crowned with a couple of fruit trees and are places where sunlight could enter easily."[5] Two or three families, who feel close to each other, live together where they feel more secure and support each other. Kitchen and living spaces are shared between the families and each family resides in a separate room.[6] Small public squares with a tree and a public fountain reflect the traditional Ottoman square concept. Fountains are elements still actively used by the residents and maintain their character as gathering spaces. Open spaces, called "*bostan*" (vegetable garden) by the locals, are used for football games, weddings and ceremonies, and function as spaces of socialisation. Cultural activities take place along the streets and proceed in the manner of a ceremonial parade.

Neighbourhood and community are the micro social units within urban space and both units, distinctive in their structures, are elements that organise everyday urban life—class, ethnic and other cultural identity. They represent an intertwined social network, much more than a simple physical structure. They can play an emancipating role through the networks or collaborations they trigger within everyday life, in order to remain an active element, resisting the oppressive mainstream global power.[7] From the perspective of Ottoman cities, the neighbourhood unit—*mahalle*—is a unique definition of a spatial community. According to Behar, "Ever since the early sixteenth century, the urban fabric of the residential areas of intramural Istanbul has consisted of a topographical location for centuries. These *mahalles* were usually not very populous, nor did they cover a wide area"; as *mahalles* are common in Istanbul, Behar explains their importance and how they continue to exist: "… these urban neighbourhood units were at all times perceived as an important protective and cohesive unit immediately surrounding the family and the household.[8] They fostered a durable sense of local identity and cohesion." The local identity also contributes to and protects the solidarity.

This is exactly the case of Sulukule, a *mahalle*—with a specific identity, which is not only an ethical identity but also a spatial organisation, and has influenced the community network and social solidarity and has embodied the street life for centuries. The demolishment by the municipality means that this unique lifestyle is being lost forever.

Aslı Kıyak İngin is an architect and Pelin Tan a sociologist and art historian, both are based in Istanbul.

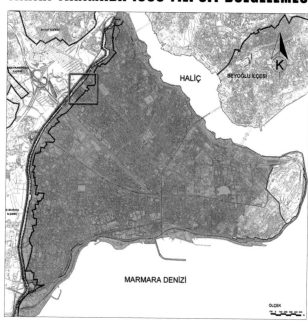

TARİHİ YARIMADA 1995 YILI SİT BÖLGELEMESİ

OPPOSITE

Demolition of the building which served as a venue for Sulukule children's workshops on 27 January 2009 at 7:30am.

ABOVE

The Sulukule district in Istanbul.

HUMAN RIGHTS

THE POPULATION OF THE SLUMS IN ITALIAN CITIES

Fabrizio Floris

It was the best of times,
it was the worst of times,
it was the spring of hope,
it was the winter of despair,
we had everything before us,
we had nothing before us.

Charles Dickens[1]

SLUMS

"Slum" is a term that evokes far-away lands and distant times like those described by Dickens or Kapuschinski, but slums are a constant and growing presence in Italy. In this country, according to estimates, there are some 6000 settlements of this kind.[2] The existence of these places has nothing to do with the pleasure of living in the open air, but is fundamentally economic in nature: the housing market following liberalisation and the growing population of immigrants with no access to social services or welfare support. The high cost of buying a house and high rents, the absence of support and the lack of alternatives push families—for this phenomenon is a crisis for families—to make their own shelters for the night. One day's work with a few wooden beams, plastic sheets, a bit of metal or glass, and the house is done. This is a single room in which to sleep at night and to host friends during the day, while the kitchen is outside. This is what happens in city spaces, in the midst of what remains of urban green spaces, among the plants; in marginal areas, steep slopes, under railway bridges, on the edges of the cities, but most often along the rivers, *by the rivers of Babylon*, the great city, because only there exists a horizon of opportunity that no other place can offer.

It is within large cities that slums develop and grow, complex cities that in microcosm reflect many of the contradictions that characterise the life of the planet. These are *world-cities* that swallow up the traditional divides that separate the world. North and south, east and west are here and live only a few metres apart. Many of the contradictions that characterise life all over the world can be seen in cities. They are places divided by many borders, the simple crossing of which produces a sense of passage from one frontier to another.[3] As Park stated, "a city grows to expand, but is characterised by selection and segregation" (Park 1967). Certainly the city has always had an elevated level of social stratification that is reflected in its architecture and its urban nature, but one can speak of

segregation to the extent that passage from one zone to another is actually impeded (Fitoussi, 2005). "Social mobility, in fact, is translated into spatial mobility" (Zorbaugh, 1929). Frontiers have not, therefore, disappeared as was thought upon the fall of the Berlin wall, but are constantly redefined. Today they do not exist any longer between east and west, or north and south, but inside cities (as if they were sovereign states), where upper class districts are strongly distinct from lower class suburbs. However, these frontiers do not only represent a barrier, but can also indicate a passage, a meeting point. The frontier, as Marc Augé explains, points at the same time to the presence of others and to the possibility of joining them. For this reason, frontiers do not disappear, but are redesigned.

CAMPS AND FRONTIERS

In the Western imagination, the word "camp" has undergone a kind of evocative slip. In Italian, *campo* means both "camp" in its English sense, and "field", a place without houses, where things grow, but without human settlement. "Camp" evokes a provisory sort of habitation, something interrupting normal life in a provisory fashion, somewhere where it should not be. Thus "if a place can be defined as relational, historical and concerned with identity, then a space which cannot has defined as relational or historical or concerned with identity will be a non-place", write Marc Augé (1995, p. 77): shopping malls, large stations, airports, playgrounds, tourist resorts, and also camps (nomad, refugee…), identical "places", indistinguishable in their geographic location, whether they be north or south or east, with the same structures, dynamics, and types of relationships. The metaphor and conceptualisation of Augé permit us to go beyond and to attempt a comparative analysis between the city and the camp: to create a narrative journey straddling an academic study and the pragmatism of experience or, as Sennet (1990) would say, "the conscience of the eye".

In the first place, the camps, of whatever kind (nomad, refugee…), fit within the definition of 'slums' according to which every space characterised by "overpopulation, temporary or informal habitation, reduced access to running water and toilets and a vague definition of property rights" (UN-Habitat 2003) can be considered a slum.[4]

On the basis of this definition, it has been estimated that the population of the slums, more than 250 thousand in the world, was in 2001 at least 921 million people. Today the inhabitants of such places represent 5.6 per cent of the Italian population, 78.2 per cent of the urban population of less-developed countries and a sixth of the citizens of the planet (Global Urban Observatory 2006, p. 77). Obviously the so-called 'nomad' camps fall into this category.

The camps are particularly interesting for what they say about the social dynamics that shape our cities. It could be said, in fact, that they redefine the city as did the industrialisation of the 1960s: they tell us right away what the city is. They are like the desert, which gives form to places it works against (Calvino 1993). Certainly the camps are not part of the city, even though they are contained within the city's perimeter; neither are they countryside or suburbs. They bear no resemblance to any kind of suburb, though theoretically they might be seen as an "abraded" suburb, a place where every service, form of infrastructure, and link with the city has been eliminated.[5] Camps march in step with a beat set by the masses. Rom, Sinti, Kalè, Manouches and Romanichals can leave different stories, different miseries, different redemptions behind them, but they will always be considered "masses" (Said 2002)–almost in order to represent the opposite, complementary and dialectic, of that society of individuals that much of contemporary sociology talks about. Here we do not find individuals–Gustavo, Giovanni, Palau, Blanko–just the generic and inequivocal "Gypsies" (Rahola 2006, p. 17). Their principal characteristic is their permanent transit through temporary places in a sort of extra-territoriality, often indistinguishable from place names because they are "in the place", not "of the place".

For this reason the camps represent a border, a "distinction that translates itself into space" (Cella 2005, p. 13), which provides an extraordinary principle of reinforcement, helping to unify that which it surrounds, merely by the fact of existing.[6] The camps, like borders, in the moment in which they become separate from the exterior, unite (or make more united) that which is enclosed within them.[7] Thus, while in the cities law and explicit regulations prevail, in the camps traditions and informal habits–that is, unwritten rules–dominate.[8]

It might thus be suggested that the camps are communities, according to the definition of Tonnies, in which reciprocity prevails, while in the cities redistribution and the market have the upper hand (Polanyi 1977). Problems come about through the close connection between these two types of settlement.

It is as if the boundary between the "rural world" and the "urban world" had been diminished, but only in terms of geographical proximity. While the camps have their basis in the ground, the city aims for the sky. In the camps, as in Medieval cities, there is an intimate unition between work and domestic life, without a functional division of space, while in the cities separation is the norm, the house is a private space, and production and exchange take place elsewhere. This contrast between community places (Redfield 1973, p. 9) and places for society mark the border between the camps and the city. The camp is not a neutral physical location, but a family place: it is where daily social and economic life is organised. The "camp", indeed, goes from being a "rest area for nomads to being a term which indicates a local community, 'those who are around the city'. The two environments remain separate precisely because the camp is not a physical place, but a familial one" (Salza 2003, p. 80). The spatial placement of the habitations of the camp is the mirror of its net of relationships: "The position of the shanties indicates familial relationships, and relations of neighbours and larger family groups precisely" (Salza 2003, p. 83). It could be said that "the camp is the family" that follows you wherever you go, and for this reason "I would say that it is our homeland, in fact we are always at home and always foreigners".[9] To understand them better, let us try to go into the camps themselves.

CAMPS AND SLUMS

At the edges of every Italian city exists a slum zone exclusively occupied by nomads of various origins. In the eyes of the rest of the city, it is mysterious, dangerous, depressing, and the outsider who ventures inside goes in the blink of an eye from a familiar world to one completely unknown. The statistics show that here the level of juvenile delinquency is high, that criminal behaviour is prevalent among adults, and that services are nonexistent. From this point of view, the inhabitants of the slums appear only as clients of social assistance, people under inquest in criminal cases, or undifferentiated members of the masses. However, something is wrong with this picture: it lacks human beings (Whyte 1961, pp. 9–10). "The greater part of sociological literature and the media tends to consider the inhabitants of the slums in terms of social problems and not of an organised social system" (Whyte 1961, p. 367). In fact, the problem of the Italian slums is not marked by a lack of organisation, but rather of the impossibility (or difficulty) that these harmonise with surrounding societal structures (Whyte 1961, p. 351). Nomads, like Italians in 1920s America, are considered the least desirable immigrants (Whyte 1961, p. 352).

They live principally in the so-called nomad camps which can be compared, following the analysis of Wirth (1928), to the former ghettos for Jews, which are analogous to the segregation of lepers in colonies, or the insane in madhouses; belonging to the group called nomads is often seen as a hereditary malady, a sign of ignominy, and the camps are a means of avoiding the contagion, breaking off communication, and blocking social integration and cultural assimilation, to isolate the group socially (Wirth 1928, p. XV). In all these cases, the place outweighs the person.

The principal characteristic of these settlements is not poverty, violence, unemployment, or even architectural decay. Their fundamental characteristic is their invisibility (Gauss 2004). The slums are here beside us, but we cannot even see them. No one knows anything, only that "that place is where Gypsies are". No one can tell anything about the occupants of these areas, and everything that anyone knows is just what he or she has always heard from someone else, who has heard it from someone else. We pass by these places, but we cannot see them. It is as if the slums were surrounded by a ghostly wall that separates one world from another, or rather a cloak that renders them invisible. Every day thousands of people pass by the slum of Strada Aeroporto in Turin or that of via Barzaghi in Milan without ever venturing inside, as if they were foreign lands, and in their own turn the inhabitants of the slums perceive everyone not living there (or not having friends there) as outsiders. It is as if there were two cities: that of the best of times and that of the worst of times, that of the spring and that of the winter, the city with a future and that which lacks one. These are two cities which "cannot become neighbours, even with the best intentions" (Park 1929, p. XIX).

Social mobility, as is well-known, is translated into spatial mobility. In slum areas there is a level of deprivation that permits no social mobility within them. In these areas without development, areas not considered "improvable", the one thing people can do to better their living conditions is to leave. In essence these are camps or slums, and must remain so.

The territorial segregation of a group is always the expression of its social marginalisation, and marginalisation is nothing but exclusion from centres of social life, from decision-making groups, and from centres of the dominant culture (Wirth 1928, p. XV). The prejudice that excludes nomads from full participation in social

PREVIOUS PAGE
Roma settlement in Aliveri Nea Ionia, Volos, photographed by Maria Papadimitriou during the EU-Roma workshops at the University of Thessaly in Greece.

TOP
A massive demonstration against the inhabitants of a Roma settlement under the flyover bridge in Ponticelli, brought attention to the slum and concluded in a fire, under the unmoving eyes of the unarmed police.

BOTTOM
Woman warming herself in front of a home in Salviati, Italy.

life contributes to the maintenance of the excluded group and guarantees the continuation of its culture. Thus there are internal and external forces that contribute to the maintenance of the camp, working in remarkable harmony; the "force" of tradition links up with the constant pressure of the external world.[10]

Clearly, after one's family has lived in the camps for generations it is not easy to leave "merely because other doors are open", because isolation from the external world has come to seem a law of existence (Wirth 1928, pp. 68–69).

The Roma flow into the camps for the same reasons that the Moroccans live in Porta Palazzo in Turin, and the Chinese on the Esquiline in Rome…. Every population is attracted by areas that relate to its economic position and cultural traditions. Every community looks for its own habitat in a similar way to that used by plants and animals. Each looks for its native food, its native language….

The physical difference that separates the nomad camps from those of the majority population is at the same time a measure of the social distance between the two and a means by which that distance can be maintained.

In this context an individual who dares to fraternise with outsiders does so at the risk of being excommunicated by his or her own group, without being sure of a welcome in the other group (Wirth 1928, p. 224).

The camp, in fact, well expresses the meaning of social conditioning. It is very difficult to stay outside certain ways of thinking or acting, just as in many popular quarters a career of deviancy comes about because it is all that "the market offers. If your neighbour lives by theft, your brother does the same, your cousin… and if all these people are also physically close to you, what else can you do? How can you make an independent choice? Obviously this should be considered in conjunction with the difficulties of work and school integration that Gypsies must face in our society. This, too, is an argument that returns to the theme of "if a person lives in a shanty, if one is unemployed it is clear that he or she will turn to theft,

but if you give him or her a job, a house… you'll see, that person will not steal".[11]

From all this, what results is self-segregation, the "closing in" of oneself in the privacy of one's own family and one's own camp. There are no important external relationships.

For this reason, the journey from a camp to a house is extremely problematic because it implies the abandonment of a familiar and generally protective environment for one that is isolated and hostile, like a house, which is, moreover, economically very costly, while in the camp one pays nothing.

As between religions and lay society, here too the conflict is of values. Perhaps greater attention and more resources could lay bare and reduce the conflict, revealing the fact that behind the conflict of values there is merely a need for more resources and more welfare, but the outcome is not guaranteed. Communities, as Weber has said (1962), do not become "societies" until they develop modern-style institutions or, in this case, accept the institutions that exist already.

In some camps, such institutions are perceived as invasive, absent, and hostile. The police, for instance, are an enemy and for even the most "lay" of nomads they are at best a hindrance, not the body that protects and guarantees the safety of citizens. This is because in the camps two levels of problem lie one on top of the other: first, that the camps are places occupied by a marginalised minority (or one that does not want to integrate), and second, that they are often occupied by persons and families dedicated to illegal activities. This is a problematic mix that assigns a criminal subculture to the minority culture, two elements that close off the psyche of each inhabitant. They are like "monoethnic Scampias" which reproduce themselves in a vicious cycle: ways of thinking, welfare, and destiny.[12] However, it is not like this everywhere. Indeed, apart from the architectural aspect, these settlements have much in common with cities (density, heterogeneity, and size, as Wirth has said). Here there are both significant analogies and important differences. What such settlements all have in

common is a way of life that does not conform to standards, but culture, expectations, objectives, style, and mentality make each settlement a place apart. This is also apparent in the construction of the buildings. Some are well-kept and clean, others on the verge of collapse. There are some settlements where the inhabitants live there by choice and would never move to an apartment, and others where the occupants feel transitory and whose goal is a more permanent home. Every settlement contains different types of population with different origins, characteristics, and expectations. Some who live there do so to live frugally and to send money to their children at university in their home countries, some do so to save money in order to build or buy a house, and some do so because they find greater protection for their illicit activities there. To sum up all these different populations under the spectre evoked by the word nomad is superficial. It is like seeing merely the aesthetic aspect of the problem, the shanties. But inside those shanties are people and groups that have nothing to do with each other whatsoever. Some are rich, some are poor, or very poor, some are workers, others are thieves, some have lived there for years, others for months. Some settlements, in fact, have a continual population flux because its population changes quickly, while others have had the same people living there for 30 years.

One could say that there exists slums of desperation and slums of hope, because for some the slums are merely a zone of passage toward the city while for others it is the final destination. Some develop a "culture of the slums" because their social values are regulated principally by the internal circumstances of the settlement and not by the outside world. Others, although living in the slums, do not take on its "values"

and keep the outside world as a constant reference point. It is useful to specify that these places run the risk of becoming a dead end for those who live there.

Both camps and slums exist. The first are often communities, while in the slums fragmentation, disorganisation, and the absence of social cohesion are the norm (Jones 1993, pp. 157–63). This is also visible in the physical appearance of the places: camps are compact, linear, and when space permits, houses are distributed in a circular form with all the doors facing the central area. In the slums there is no unity of any kind. More than considering the occupants of camps and slums as social problems, it is useful for our ends to examine the social system of these places.

From a more analytical perspective it is possible to observe that some nomad camps take the form of slums, but from a social and cultural viewpoint they are villages. The camps, in fact, are a particular type of slum, as they display all the characteristics of the latter–instability, fragmentation, absence (that is, what it lacks is what defines it)–but with one telling detail, social cohesion and recognised and representative forms of leadership, in both positive and negative terms.

In both the camps and the slums the cost of living is low, as is the quality of life. It is not that it costs less to live in a camp or a slum, because purchases are made in the city where the prices are defined, but because an occupant of a camp or a slum simply lives at a lower level. Furthermore, camps and slums are more or less "scalable" places, where social mobility is either possible or absent. Following Stokes' model (1962, pp. 189–194), it can be said that in the camps mobility via legal means is frozen and impossible, and it is

enough to note that the same family groups can be found in the same place over many years. In contrast with the slums, though only where the leadership is not dedicated to illegal activities, social advancement is possible in the camps, and for this reason social workers state "that one works better in the unlawful areas", as there they find people open to ways of social integration. In the camps, as one worker of long experience says, "I often happened to hear phrases like 'We're fine like this, it's you who want us to integrate… there's another way to live, and it's our way'."[13]

The slum is the "home" of the poor and of foreigners, while the camp is neither one nor the other. In fact, many of the inhabitants of camps are Italian, and anything but poor. Neither place is integrated with the city, and in both one can find desperation and hope, while in the camps immobility is the norm, a frozen transitory quality that is often intentionally chosen.

Once again according to the model of Stokes, it can be said that while the slums of hope tend to "disappear" over time, or to house another population, the slums of desperation tend to last. The slums of hope are landing-places, inhabited by a population with work skills often acquired beforehand, and the cognitive ability to move around and seize opportunities offered in the marketplace. Their formation depends on the rate of immigration and on the immigrants' level of integration; in practice, with policies aimed at welfare the problem can be overcome (Table 1, A).

The slums of desperation are places where criminal leaders, via various forms of exploitation, block the social growth of the inhabitants, who, lacking documents and resources (in terms of culture, economy, and social awareness…), are forced into

Temporary shelter in a factory demolition site in Snia, Milan.

an almost feudal dependency on the chief. Indeed, the most minimal self-advancement is punished with expulsion. Here social mobility is possible only insofar as it is possible to free oneself from constriction, when there are no important socio-cultural blocks (Table 1, B).

The camps where a merely economic integration prevails without an accompanying cultural integration falls into the category of model C in the plan below. There are socio-cultural blocks that impede an exit from the camps from being perceived as other than an element of desperation; some authorised areas form part of this typology. In the end, the camps where there is no economic integration and at the same time socio-economic impediments do exist that do not favour an exploration of alternatives may be considered places of desperation and immobility. This immobility can be favoured both by subjective factors (a low level of education, cultural factors…) and by objective factors (absence of documents, absence of work opportunities…) (Table 1, D). Not least, each one of these typologies would merit different social policies (Calabrò 2008, pp. 70–71).

TABLE 1 TYPOLOGIES OF SLUMS

	HOPE	DESPERATION
SOCIAL MOBILITY	A	B
SOCIAL/SPATIAL IMMOBILITY	C	D

Source: Stokes 1962, p. 189.

From the analysis undertaken to this point, it can be said that temporary settlements do not present a cohesive social structure, a solid hierarchy, or recognised and legitimate forms of leadership; "Each camp, it can be said, arranges itself in its own way."

The settlements under analysis present significantly different characteristics from the inside, such that it can be said that some are simply slums without social cohesion, while others are more like camps, in the sense of non-cities, where "face to face" relationships are the norm (Hannerz 1992, p. 56), but only between members of the settlement. In the camps oral communication tends to dominate, and the members of the community are very similar to each other in their ways of both thinking and behaving. Moreover the conventions that bind individuals together are verbal rather than contractual. Social relations are conceived of and categorised in terms of family bonds, these being the only factors that differentiate them: "relations are the typical figures of reference for every experience". The camps are, thus, very similar to a folk society where concepts of moral value are associated with ways of thinking and acting. We can, in this sense, define the camps as urban villages, rural communities inserted into an urban environment, but which follow the rules of the community, or rather, the three original forms of community: the family network, the community of place, and friendships all join up here. One lives in the same place with one's own friends and family members (Tonnies 1963, pp. 45–46).[14]

For this reason the passage from the camp to the city runs the risk of being a moment of *anomie*, a social vacuum of values and rules.[15]

However, while the camps might be considered "fated" communities, in contrast the inhabitants of the slums are able to integrate themselves more easily, given that they do not have strong relationships to protect. One might, indeed, argue that both the camps and the slums represent a sort of extraterritoriality, outside society.

Finally, camps and slums are not the city, and they are denied their right to exist and to call themselves cities. They are clandestine places in contrast with the city, and they live on a different level, in both a strict and a figurative sense. While the city "stands above", economically bound to the rest of the world and often in horizontal communication with cities of equal grade rather than vertically with the slums down below, the clandestine city (the camp or slum) is intimately linked to the earth, because every day it must fight to have a piece of land to build on.

From an aesthetic viewpoint the modern skyscrapers of Milan and the shanties of via Barzaghi are the symbol of these two cities, that of the slums and that of the palaces, which, like the mountains, never meet.[16]

Fabrizio Floris is a Doctor of Sociology from the University of Turin, Department of Social Sciences.

GREECE

In Thessaly, the degree of integration of Roma Gypsies in the social security system is still very low, and studies indicate that many Roma are unaware of their rights in the field of medical care and lack confidence in the public health system. Notwithstanding serious medical problems aggravate the situation further although positive steps have been taken to assist the communities, such as regular monitoring of children's vaccination and increasing women doctors in hospitals.

TOP

Dwelling in Tyrnavos, Thessaly, Greece.

BOTTOM

Remains of a Gypsy settlement in Aliveri, Nea Ionia, Volos.

TRIBONIANO
ITALY

The historic settlement of Triboniano is squeezed between a railway track, cemetery and a container storage. Police and the NGO Casa della Carità are supervising the area with strict patrols allowing families to leave and enter, collecting rent and electricity due. To be able to reside in the settlement each family signed a protocol of conduct, which is very problematic for Roma. They must demonstrate they are working, that their children go to school, that their visa is valid. If any of these obligations are not fulfilled they will be removed right away.

TOP
View of the wall dividing the container storage from the new settlement.

BOTTOM
View of the Triboniano streets.

OPPOSITE TOP
Aerial view of the Triboniano settlement before renovation, visible is the container storage and cemetery.
Courtesy of www.bing.com/maps

OPPOSITE CENTRE
View of the new Triboniano settlement.

ASSESSING THE ROMANIAN SITUATION
IGNORANCE OR RACISM?

Florin Botonogu

According to UNDP data, the infant mortality for the Roma population of Romania, the largest minority here, estimated at around 1.8 million people, is four times higher than the country's average. The percentage of Roma who do not have access to running water or sewage is 68 per cent while the number of square metres per person is reported to be 14, compared to 32 in the majority communities situated in the near proximity. The most evident form of exclusion is reflected in their living conditions. Poor housing, segregation, ghettoisation, and a lack of access to public services are just a few of their difficulties. Their socio-economic situation is continuously degrading, while the measures for its improvement are still on paper. When it comes to implementation the local authorities become less interested, if not reluctant.

Although poor Roma neighbourhoods can be encountered all over the country and are more and more visible, they are not recognised or brought into the discussion by local authorities, nor by the academics or central government. It is only when it comes to ethnic conflict or evictions that these communities are in the public eye, most of the time putting all responsibility on the victims.

In the absence of a state policy regarding housing for poor people, the local authority remains the main stakeholder responsible for improving the living conditions in Romanian slums. With no clear provisions preventing discrimination or slum formation, the local governments adopt a whole range of measures that lead to unsustainable development and segregation. It is true that solving housing problems requires a lot of financial resources and a lot of consultation and coordination. It is also true that there may not be a lot of resettlement options. Economic decline usually triggers economic migration to urban areas, which increases the pressure on the cities to accommodate new arrivals with a low status. But all these aspects cannot explain many of the housing solutions taken by the local authorities in Romania. There is a huge gap between their attempts to include poor people's housing in the development of the city and the obviously unsuitable, even illegal, decisions they take. This gap cannot be explained only by the lack of expertise, although this is a major factor.

The difference between the declared intentions and the reality of segregation and ghettoisation can only be explained by political choice and prejudice. Social housing cannot be sustainable unless it involves a process of consultation with the entire community and joint decision. In Romania, and not only here, placing Roma communities on the margins of the city or in isolated locations seems to be the preferred urban development paradigm. Instead of realising that creating ghettoes is a risk for the entire local community, local authorities believe that relocation is the magic solution.

It is very easy to label an attitude or behaviour as racism and point a finger at the disregard and lack of expertise of the town planners in Romania towards the problem of the poor. It is difficult to cite racism here, but easy to hint at the widely spread attitudes and actions towards Roma neighbourhoods, by describing different ways of discrimination they suffer.

SEGREGATION

The first segregation case that became notorious in Romania was the "Speranta" ("Hope") neighbourhood. Piatra Neamt is a cosy town in Northeast Romania, surrounded by gorgeous mountains and hills. In 2001, the mayor publicly declared his intention to create a ghetto for Roma outside the city. They were to be resettled in a chicken farm that was supposed to be surrounded by barbed wire and permanently guarded by gendarmes and dogs. Due to the strong reaction of the Roma NGOs and international organisations, the mayor had to change his intentions and to create an ethnically mixed neighbourhood. Several Romanians received apartments in nice blocks of flats while Roma lived just nearby, in the chicken farm.

Another well-known case is the three metres high wall of Tarlungeni, Brasov County. It was built by a local landlord in order to separate the Romanians and Hungarians from the Roma. Although segregation is more than obvious, civil servants consider this high wall just a fence around a property. In Dorohoi, in North Romania, Roma who were living in the historical centre of the city were prevented from accessing the city centre by the blocking of the main entrance in the common courtyard. They had to use the back gate and walk around for almost one kilometre to reach the centre.

Segregation also has historical roots, dating back to the Communist regime. At Bolovanu village we can observe the results of a segregation process produced forty years ago. At that time, the communists responsible displaced a Roma community 40 kilometres away from on a hill between two villages. Practically, they don't belong to any administrative unit now and of course no village wants to incorporate them. This case is very similar to what the Roman authorities did under Mr Weltroni where some communities were removed to the remote area of Castel Romano, several kilometres away from other human settlements.

Miercurea Ciuc is another well documented place for the segregation of Roma. There are four Roma communities around the city that are completely separated, have poor access to infrastructure and are totally abandoned by the authorities. Segregation is not the result of an explicit policy in Romania and its presence is not even recognised by the local authorities, nor is it an issue of concern for the government. But it's a silently expanding phenomenon with major consequences in the short- and long-term, both for the people and the entire city.

IMPROPER LIVING CONDITIONS

The debate on discrimination in living conditions for Roma is based on the huge discrepancy between the situation of housing in these communities and the neighbouring communities. The most important services that are missing or underdeveloped are: public utilities (water, sewage, electricity, access roads) public services like schools, cultural centres, markets and community facilities (public phones, public electricity, facilities for people with disabilities, playgrounds). But the main thing is that many houses are in a very bad condition, sometimes endangering the life of inhabitants. In fact, Romanian authorities do not even know the number of poor housing communities and the type of intervention needed for each one.

Even if it's hard to prioritise when it comes to basic needs, the first interventions should be related to excluding health risk factors by introducing running water and waste management systems. In the Valea Rece (Cold Valley) community situated in Tîrgu Mures city there is only one source of water for 1,500 people. In Dorohoi there were three public toilets for 360 persons. Most often toilets are situated in the vicinity of water sources. There are major problems with garbage collection, not to mention communities that are situated in the garbage pits or on their margins. Improper living conditions are regarded primarily as a poverty issue with the main responsibility usually falling on the victims but if we fail to consider it equally a human rights issue we will only witness its development.

ENVIRONMENTAL RACISM

Despite the clear provisions of the Romanian law forbidding human settlements close to garbage pits or other pollution sources, there are many communities in Romania situated in such an environment. There are two main causes for that: rural migration for survival opportunities and the disposition of the local authorities. The most well known case is Pata Rat (Cluj County). Here, like in many other places, Roma sort garbage and sell the recuperated materials and this is often their only source of income. There are plans for closing this garbage pit in 2010 and to move Roma in new blocks of flats, but this should be completed by other measures for their economic recovery. Maybe labelling this situation as racism, as nobody forces them to stay there, is not that obvious, but the fact that in the whole country only Roma communities live in these conditions and the tolerance of the cities to the huge health risks, child labour and general misery represents, for sure, a different treatment by the local authorities towards these groups. Truth is that they have no other option; they have been denied any other job or place to settle.

Often the local authorities themselves are the ones that relocate Roma communities on polluted soil or very close to pollution sources. In Miercurea Ciuc, a small city in the centre of Romania, 12 families had been resettled in 2004 just near the city's sewage factory. Even if it is a very clear action of discrimination against Roma, sanctioned by Romanian National Council against Discrimination and in the attention of European Court for Human Rights, the local authorities do not think of it in these terms. Nearly one hundred people have been living for five years in eight small barracks and 12 shacks, surrounded by a permanent acrid smell, with only one source of water and four public toilets. At this point personal or collective prejudice plays a major role in designing housing solutions for poor Roma communities.

INSECURE TENURE AND ILLEGAL EVICTIONS

The insecurity of tenure is high in poor Roma settlements. Lack of property documents on the land or of any legal form of occupancy has historical roots but the intervention of the state to alleviate this situation is very timid. Security of tenure is first an individual duty, but the complexity of the legal solution requires some facilitation from the state authorities. Many of the illegal Roma communities are exposed to evictions.

A consequence of it is ethnic conflicts. Starting with the beginning of the 90s (Bolintin, Hadareni) and continuing until summer of 2009 (Sanmartin and Sancraieni), violent conflicts between Roma and the majority population have ended in burning their houses or simply devastating or forcing Roma to leave the village. Insecurity of tenure makes legal interventions very difficult in these situations, if not impossible. Again the indifference of the local authorities combined with the few choices the Roma have form a vicious cycle.

Regarding illegal evictions, there are not enough provisions for respecting fundamental human rights like making evictions resulting in homelessness in the winter time. Usually evictions result in segregation or homelessness. Compact Roma communities are slowly pushed to the margins of or outside the city. The scarcity of legal provisions and the lack of law enforcement make illegal evictions very easy for local authorities. The huge ignorance of these topics is what is specific today in Romania despite their spread. Prejudice and racist attitudes against Roma find the most concrete form of manifestation in housing. Until now, the very few actions proved to be unsustainable, even inappropriate for community development. Will the raising of awareness and knowledge lead to a diminishing of the current racism?

CASTEL ROMANO
ROME ITALY

Castel Romano is a settlement, known as the "container camp", outside the city of Rome. It is a legal camp housing approximately 800 people, authorised, funded and constructed by the city of Rome in 2005, and located on a nature reserve belonging to the region of Lazio.

Castel Romano was built to house the former residents of the 25 year old campsite Vicolo Savini, situated in the city centre of Rome and which was closed in September 2005 due to poor sanitary conditions. The Roma were moved into tents on the Castel Romano site for what was intended to be two months, but extended to eight, while container units and a basic infrastructure of electricity, water, gas, and sewage was installed.

The Castel Romano community is mostly composed of families from the former Yugoslavia, many having immigrated to Rome before the Bosnian conflicts of the early 1990s and others who arrived during the war. Almost all Roma who are resident at Castel Romano wish to become Italian citizens, but have found the status difficult to attain. Many still hold citizenship in their country of origin and since in Italy citizenship is inherited, many second and even third-generation Roman-born Roma are technically foreign citizens, making work permits, residence permits, and even driving licenses very difficult to obtain.

Castel Romano is the largest legal Roma camp in Italy and is the first of four or five "mega-camps" proposed by the city to house Roma. The city's mayor at the time called Castel Romano a "Village of Solidarity". All proposed locations for the mega-camps are, like Castel Romano, outside the Grande Raccordo Anulare (GRA), the ring road that surrounds the city.

Castel Romano is managed by Impegno, a non-profit organisation, which coordinates emergency housing. Impegno works in collaboration with a Roma rights organisations and ARCI, who serve as liaisons to the community. All these organisations have representatives present in container offices (prefabricated units) on site. ARCI is also responsible for arranging transportation for the children to schools and acts as liaison between schools and families.

The problems of habitation that face the Roma in Italy are inextricably linked to problems of culture, economy, citizenship, racism, and human and civil rights but habitation is not only the issue of decent housing and infrastructure, but also the surrounding social and psychological environment.

Case study by LAN and Iowa State University Rome.

OPPOSITE TOP
The former Roma settlement in Vicolo Savini in the city centre of Rome.

BOTTOM
The interior of a prefabricated home in the new settlement of Castel Romano.

TOP
Panorama of the central plaza in
Castel Romano.

BOTTOM
View of a burnt prefabricated house.

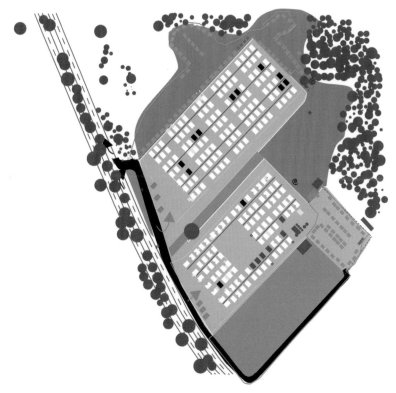

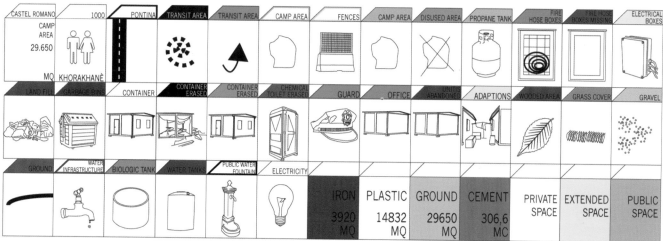

CASTEL ROMANO CAMP AREA 29.650 MQ KHORAKHANÈ	1000	PONTINA	TRANSIT AREA	TRANSIT AREA	CAMP AREA	FENCES	CAMP AREA	DISUSED AREA	PROPANE TANK	FIRE HOSE BOXES	FIRE HOSE BOXES MISSING	ELECTRICAL BOXES
LAND FILL	GARBAGE BINS	CONTAINER	CONTAINER ERASED	CONTAINER ERASED	CHEMICAL TOILET ERASED	GUARD	OFFICE	UNITS ABANDONED	ADAPTIONS	WOODED AREA	GRASS COVER	GRAVEL
GROUND	WATER INFRASTRUCTURE	BIOLOGIC TANK	WATER TANKS	PUBLIC WATER FOUNTAIN	ELECTRICITY	IRON 3920 MQ	PLASTIC 14832 MQ	GROUND 29650 MQ	CEMENT 306,6 MC	PRIVATE SPACE	EXTENDED SPACE	PUBLIC SPACE

OPPOSITE

A municipal school bus arrives early in the morning to collect the Roma children, but a mixture of family problems and racial pressures prevent the large majority from attending.

TOP

EU-Roma Mapping of the population, ground cover, layout of containers and amenities of the Castel Romano settlement. Study conducted with students from Iowa State University Rome.

BOTTOM

The only source of drinking water for 800 residents.

TOP
A kitchen inside one of the prefabricated homes.

BOTTOM
Water collected from the communal pump.

OPPOSITE
Alleyways become gardens and laundry rooms as an extension of the home, a typical feature of Roma living.

GIUGLIANO CAMPANIA NAPLES ITALY

The "Camp" of Giugliano is an unofficial "spontaneous" settlement accommodating roughly 500 people of whom 50 per cent are adolescents and children and divided into 85 families, all from former-Yugoslavia. Some have lived in Italy for more than 40 years but the majority came over to join family members already living in the area as part of the flow of migration following the 1991 Balkan war. Their culture, traditions and language are still passed on orally. Unlike the new generations, the old, who are by now parents or grand-parents, are illiterate apart from the exception of some men who claim to have learned to read and write in order to pass their driving test. The languages spoken are Romanes, Serbo-Croat and Italian. Relationships with non-Roma (principally mediators and institutions but also employers) of the area are good although contact is infrequent.

The settlement is set up as a continuous camp subdivided into 13 units. Of these camps n.s 11, 7 and 13 have been monitored (called the "Opera Nomadi" and recognised by the inhabitants), as they are substantial from the point of view of the settlement and represent a heterogeneous sample of the present situation. The remaining settlements are composed of single family units.

The settlement is located in the municipality of Giugliano, to the northwest of Naples, at the outer limits of the urban centre, on the external ring-road following the State Highway 162. Giugliano is served by suburban public transport which does not cross the area of the settlement, and is therefore reachable only by private means.

The camp, in existence since 1991, was constructed on agricultural land which is flat with both cultivated and wild green areas, as the Roma who have been there since then will confirm, and which still resembles agricultural land of the past. Later on, with the application of the General Urban Development Plan (Piano Regolatore Generale) of 2004, the Municipal Council of Giugliano assigned the land as a PIP zone (Plan for Productive Settlements) and around the settlement arose numerous industries, such as an ex-refuse collection centre and various refuse deposits, places then taken over by the legal authorities. Today they are considered as areas of "strategic interest" by the Commission of the Government for the Campania Refuse Emergency and are guarded by the army and police.

For these reasons, today the administration, by means of a private security firm (Falko Security S.R.I.S.), has created a barricade system under 24-hour surveillance, 30 metres from the entrance to the "camp".

The 13 units in the settlement, of differing character and dimension are linked together mainly by degrees of kinship (a link that applies to the whole group), or of friendship relative to the number of years spent in the camp as a permanent resident.

Each centre has its own well-defined area of control with a single entrance, others with a perimeter which is less clear and demarcated. The borders of the various units are made up of natural elements such as trees, hedges and embankments, but also of man-made elements, barriers and fences of the adjacent factories or made by the residents with recycled materials or with actual mounds of rubbish.

The settlements are connected neither to the electricity network, the water mains, nor even to the sewage system. Some of the inhabitants are hooked up informally to the electricity supply and pay a fee to the nearby factories. It's the same for the water supply. The majority supply themselves with drinking water with canisters transported individually and with generators that run on petrol for electricity. Toilet facilities are made up of a system of septic tanks or drainage ditches and are located behind the shacks at the edges of the camp in separate wooden cabins.

Winter heating is obtained from wood heaters, constructed by the residents and located in the central space of the living quarters. The heater is often also used for cooking, baking bread and for the heating of water.

The area is included in the refuse collection service but the containers are not sufficiently big for the number of users and the collection of refuse is not carried out on a regular basis. The result is that the refuse often gets burnt or collected by private companies hired directly by the residents, the latter in order to limit the possibility of the outbreak of infectious diseases and the proliferation of rats.

The desire to integrate is strong and it pushes the inhabitants to stress the similarities between their culture and ours. In that regard the families who seek to improve their living conditions are less willing to live in their own extended community.

The first generation, those who were the first to emigrate, preserve their links more with their country of birth. Only the few old people still alive spend some period of the year in the former-Yugoslavia while the new generations feel no kinship or emotional ties to those countries. The ever-present threat of expulsion from Italy gives rise to a great degree of worry and bewilderment, above all among the minors who are Italian for all intents and purposes.

The inhabitants are fundamentally sedentarised. They live in the "camp" and have no desire to move around. The main problem remains the acquisition of documentation that recognises their integration into Italian society and the possibility of offering their children a better future. The majority of children go to the primary school and some of them try to continue their schooling (technical and hotel institutions, etc.) urged on by their parents and their own desire for a more dignified life.

Sources of great malaise include: the noise pollution produced by the neighbouring factories, air pollution from the same factories and the ex-centre for refuse collection; pollution from the burnt refuse; the danger of the roads being very near their homes and the areas in which their children play; the dirt and run-off from the illegal dumping of toxic industrial waste in the immediate vicinity and the necessity to wash themselves outside which is dangerous for children.

The will to leave the neighbourhood with their families is clear, if only to have better living conditions. If splitting up allowed them to improve their individual conditions, sacrificing the proximity to the group is a compromise and strategy which would be acceptable for the need to adapt.

The wish to leave the camp as a residential structure is widespread, as is the will to identify alternatives for one's own family group, moving closer to the city to get out of a precarious and marginalised situation.

In the last few months, since the census conducted by the Ministry for the Interior, after beginning work on the construction of a new "campo nomadi" located on land bordering the area already occupied and that will be able to house 106 people and after an ordinance that the area must be cleared out for health reasons, tension is reaching very high levels. The new local administration even asked the architect in charge for an adjustment to the project—to raise the surrounding wall from an initial height of 45 centimetres to 270 cm, a real physical and visual barrier to hide the Roma settlement.

Case study LAN with Raffaella Inglese.

Camp 13
Ash soil from the
endless arson attacks.

FROM TOP TO BOTTOM

Camp 3
'Tyre dwelling', the bathroom
and the back yard.

Camp 3
Zoran's living room.

Camp 7
Building site.

Camp 13
360' view of Camp 7.

RIGHT

Map of Guilgiano showing the
different Roma camps and the
divisions of territory in between
the factories and refuse sites.

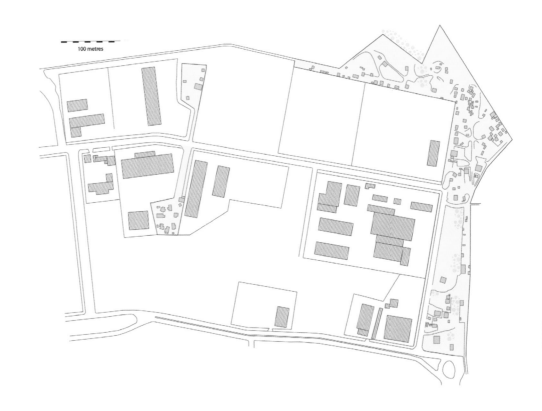

BELOW

360° view of Camp 7.

BOTTOM

Interior of a dwelling in Camp 13.

MIERCUREA
TRANSYLVANIA
ROMANIA

Miercurea Ciuc is a Transylvanian town with 42,000 inhabitants, where Romanians are a minority (14 per cent), while the majority is represented by Hungarians (82 per cent). Roma can be spotted inside the city in mixed communities and outside in separate. We visited five of these communities and encountered a variety of forms of sub-standard living conditions, discrimination, residential segregation and environmental racism.

PRIMAVERII–SPRINGTIME STREET

Spring never smells good for Roma here. Actually it's quite the opposite, as they live right near a sewage treatment plant. They used to live inside the city, in a historical building used as social housing, until 2004. The building was abandoned by the municipality as they were about to lose it in favour of its former private owner. The private owner could not intervene as he didn't have full rights to evict the tenants yet and the Roma did not maintain the building in a good condition as most of them were unemployed and about to be evicted. As a result the building degraded, the new owner ordered an expert that qualified the building as dangerous, and the community was evicted and the building demolished. There are three major drawbacks with the new location.

First, the environmental racism that is obvious for everybody but the local municipality. The norms state that the living area should be at least 300 metre away from the sewage unit. This is not the case here, as the only barrier between the houses and the reservoirs is a barbed wire fence. The fence can be easily crossed and children sometimes play near industrial devices with moving parts and insufficient electrical insulation. The health of the entire community is in danger here, not to mention the permanent odour. The National Council for Combating Discrimination has issued a fine for the local municipality (1,200 Euros), but nothing followed from the part of the Romanian authorities. The case is now at the attention of European Court of Human Rights.

The second is segregation. The unpaved access road is hardly accessible by car and when it rains even by foot. The living area is limited by a small canal leading to a pig farm which is used for washing clothes, the sewage plant and agricultural land. The centre is relatively close; you can reach it in 30 minutes by foot, as there is no public transportation. There is no planning documentation for this plot of land that is now inhabited by some 150 people.

Last but not least the living conditions are totally improper. 12 barracks were provided by the municipality at the beginning and then another 20 were built by the people. Each barrack measures ten square metres and provides shelter for 5 to 6 persons.

Although this was supposed to be a temporary settlement, after five years it is still there. There is only one source of water for the whole community and four wooden toilets provided by the local municipality, there is no sewage system, no public phones nor other public services in the surrounding area.

THE GARBAGE PIT

25 years ago when there was no garbage pit here, near the stray dog facility, a family moved here from the centre of the town, just three kilometres away from the town limits. Since then, it has grown into a small community of 25 people now housed in seven shacks, one inside the garbage pit and six on its edge.

Although their history is a bit unclear, it underlines the old and current processes of urban refurbishment without taking people into account. The local authorities' lack of interest for these people is total. Some of them do not even have identity cards; kids don't go to school as there is no transportation available. Their only source of water is a hydrant. There are no toilets and no public phones. The only job available to them and to their children is sorting the garbage for ten hours a day. The only public institution they are in contact with is the hospital but as they do not have social insurance they have to pay for every service. One of the elderly women needed surgery for a tumour; they managed to borrow money from their "employer", and this was done as a collective effort and now they have to work, according to our calculations, at least one year for free to pay the debts.

OPPOSITE

Map of Roma communities in and around Miercurea. Map by Asociatia Pentru Tranzitie Urbana.

BOTTOM

Social housing in Primaverii (Springtime Street).

OVERLEAF

There is no electricity but people still decorate their interiors with electrical appliances. The lamp has no bulbs, the TV worked once on a car battery. This home is erected on the garbage pit.

The shacks reveal the lack of most elementary building knowledge and tools. They are made of pieces of wood covered with cardboard, linoleum and other recycled materials. People are exposed to rats and fire, and every year one of the shacks burns. This is the reason they prefer to build them separately. In summer they cook outside in totally unhygienic conditions.

JIGODIN

It was economic migration that led to the formation of this community several years ago. They came from a nearby village, settled on a hill outside the city limits and received a verbal permit from the mayor to stay. He allowed them to build several houses on the Jigodin hill in a spirit of acceptance, without any following interventions. This group is formed of Hungarian Roma; the only languages they speak are Hungarian and Romany so our conversation could not take place in Romanian but in Romany. Unlike most of the Roma they don't have any idea what kind of historical subgroup they belong to.

Comparing to the previous examples we can observe that houses are built in an advanced manner, very similar to a traditional village house. Their rural background provides them basic skills for building. The shelters, though minimal, offer more protection to the inhabitants. They felt the need for a clear partition between public and private land and so they built a sort of fence, although they do not possess property documents. There is a total lack of public utilities and of interest on behalf of local authorities but they seems to do better, as they possess a horse and have also started to extend one of the houses.

SUMULEU

This is a typical neighbourhood in a Transylvanian settlement, at the end of the road, a community of around 200 Roma that came from the neighbouring villages 40 years ago. The characteristics of housing here are overcrowding and a diversity of building materials, from brick houses to shelters similar to the ones from the garbage pit. The only source of water is a pump. The electricity transformer was not fenced and this lead to an accident in 2007. The river passing behind is polluted and it is used by children for playing. They make their living from collecting garbage and recycling materials. Some of them have carts and horses.

OPPOSITE
Shelter erected on the garbage pit outside Miercurea.

ABOVE
Hungarian Roma village in Jigodin.

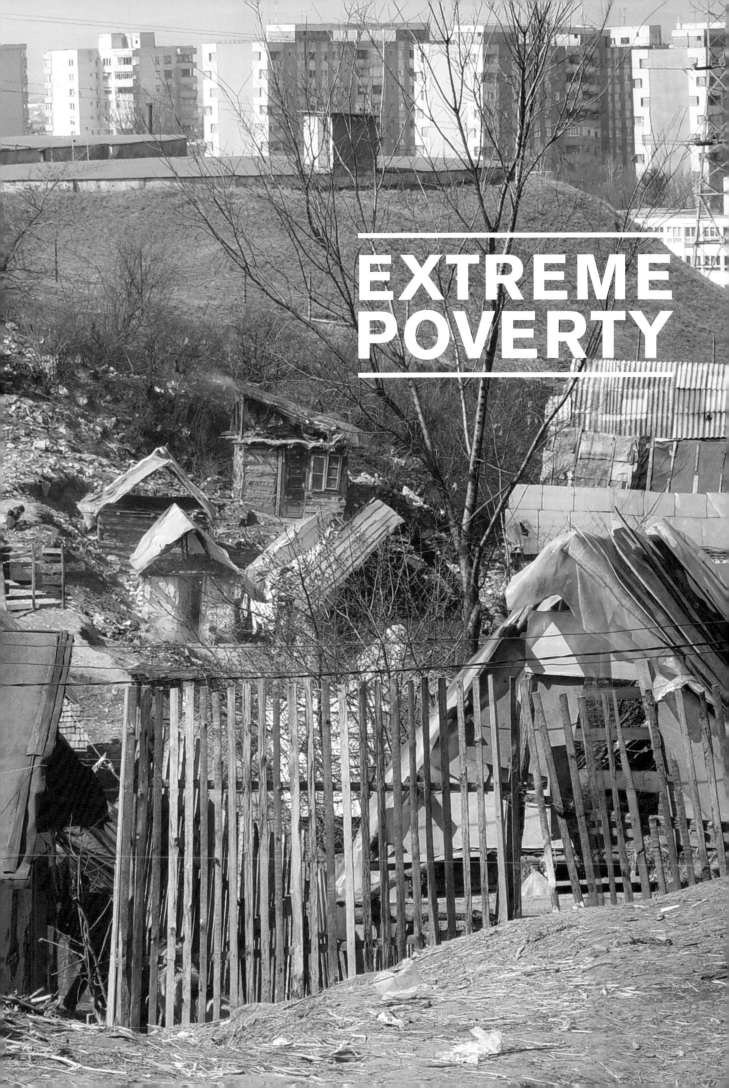

EXTREME
POVERTY

THE SHADOWS OF THE FUTURE
EAST EUROPE AND ITS NEW ROMA GHETTOES

Catalin Berescu

Many things have changed since the collapse of communism in Romania and elsewhere, some of them brutal, some more gentle, some very fast. Some have created a sense of relief, explosion of joy and an unprecedented feeling of liberty. Other things were slow and went undetected. Today, our major political and economical achievements are still measured by our capacity to put a safe distance between the socialist times and the present. We live in an era driven by a strong ethos of change, by the irrepressible will to dismantle everything that was petrified during Ceausescu, subsequently challenged by the fear to lose the old ways, the safety and familiarity of the well known gestures. I will leave aside the efficiency of the process—it is common knowledge that Romania still lags behind other recent EU members—as I am more interested in pointing at the current state of mind of both the public and, as a result, of the authorities. More than in other times and places of dramatic historic change, here, in Romania, we hate our recent past. We got rid of most of the wrongs but we are not willing to give up everything from the past because we are not quite sure what will replace it. One of these 'socialist' features is a social and ethnic mix.

DRAMATIC EQUALITY

During communism, the entire population was under control, including the Roma. At that time they were integrated within society, offered jobs and education, and often received apartments in social housing blocks of flats. Equality was key, the ruling concept that lead to uniformity and lack of social perspective, but also ensured—or perhaps, put properly, 'imposed' —a very strong safety net for the needy. Nowadays if you just mention equality in Romania you might be booed, or at least be instantly suspected to be a communist nostalgic. In the intellectual *milieu* it is *bon ton* to affirm, with a small amount of superiority, like one of our former Prime Ministers did, that "We are not equal!" It is not a sign of a poignant self-consciousness, of an arrogant individuality but merely a way to delimit from the unworthy, a way to signal the fact that you do not belong anymore to the proletarian, underperforming, egalitarian class. This idea, of a strong process of class differentiation, is further supported by the observation that charity here is just a giveaway, a donation of money or goods, a gesture of benevolence and a religious obligation, but less an involvement in concrete actions. Romanians do give to the poor and needy but it is always a gift with no or limited interaction. Most of our NGO's are run by foreigners or were created as counterparts of foreign organisations, and there is almost no grass roots activism for public causes.

However, besides the oppression of the elites and of the "imprisonment" of the possible entrepreneurs in low standard prefabricated collective dwellings, the forced equality policy had a positive side effect: a social and ethnic mix was to be found all over Romania, or at least a form of it, lacking real interaction but with plenty of strategies to adapt diversity. The shortcomings of this centralised and somehow militarised activity for Roma was that most of the traditional nomadic communities were

BELOW

Gazela is an unplanned settlement that developed informally under the large Gazela Bridge, one of the few access points to the city centre of Belgrade in former-Yugoslavia. Most of the structures are constructed from recycled materials such as wood and plastic, but the older houses are made of stone with patios and gardens. A few days before the EU-Roma visit, a fire had destroyed some shacks and families were sheltered in prefabricated structures donated by the local Red Cross.

PREVIOUS PAGE

Valea Rece, a poverty stricken community of approximately 1500 Roma on the periphery of Tîrgu Mures one of the major Transylvanian cities.

TOP
View of Gazela settlement
from the railway, Belgrade.

BOTTOM
View under the highway bridge
of Gazela settlement, Belgrade.

settled by force and many of the already settled were moved to remote areas. Integration wiped out identity, with the result being that fewer than half of the Roma are able to speak the native Romani language today. So, on the one hand, the existing ghettoes were diminished, and in fact many of them disappeared; on the other hand, the nomads were put into ethnic enclaves, with the prospect of turning them into future poverty ghettoes. As a matter of fact, some of them turned into rich ghettoes and developed a particular architectural style that proved to be a fascinating subject for international photographers.

In our struggle to restructure society and to give free initiative and individualism the place they deserved, and during the race to replace the omnipresent poverty with wealth, one side effect was not considered: the rise of extreme poverty. 50 years of imposed, finally dramatic equality are reversed in a way that is leading us now to what is often qualified, in the new *langue de bois* terminology of European reports and reportages, as dramatic inequality.

THE OLD AND THE NEW POVERTY

As soon as we start to think about poverty a profusion of cultural and personal references appear. Depending on our lectures, Dickens or Shalom Alehem, Zola or Marx, the Bible or the last Organisation for Security and Co-operation in Europe (OSCE) report, each informs a particular cultural vision on poverty. Besides that, we can actually see it, smell it and maybe get a taste of it, as the vast majority of us has experienced poverty on our own; in relative terms almost every student is poor and every family has a relative that does not do very well.

Based on that, there is a common understanding of poverty as incapacity to reach the normal standards, and a generalised sense of compassion for those affected by it. But when it comes to practical terms, of how to manage it, things are more complicated. It always starts with measuring it, which differs according to various complex econometric schemes that take into account mainly consumption and income. The key concept for understanding this layer of poverty is 'normal' and the technical expression of it is represented by different savant calculated average figures. We call this level of poverty "relative", as it varies through the years, countries and even regions and cities. The search for the average line is continuous and somehow defines the modern welfare state.[1]

There is much more under this relative level. Usually the levels are defined using the two dollars per day and one dollar per day threshold. But in functional terms, severe poverty can be defined as a chronic state of lack of resources that leads to permanent effects on a person in terms of health, education, employment, etc.[2] The destitute, the ones living in want, the ones that are living under a permanent threat of losing everything they have, including their life, are to be qualified as living in extreme poverty.

As we step down to the extreme poverty level, other cultural references are to be evoked, usually a dramatic picture of a dystrophic child in Sahel, or a squalid slum in Mumbai, Cape Town or São Paolo. Very distant places, exotic in many ways, definitely non-European. This time, however, our references are more distant. As few people have been to these places there is a strong sense of danger associated with them, predestined to be explored by fearless journalists and people with a missionary

vocation. Nevertheless, horrible smelling slums, all of them inhabited mainly by Roma, flourished in Eastern Europe in the last 20 years; from the (in)famous Lunik IX in Kosice, Slovakia, to the recently dislocated Gazela Bridge in Belgrade, or from Pata Rat, the garbage camp of Cluj, Romania, to the autonomous Fakulteta, near Sofia. We have it here, right near us, and Eastern Europeans are now exporting it to Western Europe and more and more people talk about it.

These poverty areas are combining ethnical discrimination (leading to ghettoes), with social exclusion in what we can call "new poverty". In Eastern Europe this is a relatively recent phenomenon characterised by its very persistence, and driven by multidimensional determinants. It is mostly specific to urban areas, leads to weaker family ties, non-participation and social marginalisation. It also fosters various deviant subcultures and concentrates the poor in segregated territories. If consumption poverty is decreasing as an effect of economic growth, the "new poverty" is developing as an effect of increasing inequality and weakening of social cohesion and cannot be overcome without interventions from outside.[3] (Stanculescu: 2004) New urban poverty often takes extreme forms—ethnically segregated enclaves lacking basic utilities, with difficult access, abandoned by administration but guarded like prisons by the police—characterised by their lack of connection and symbolic invisibility in relationship with the rest of the urban tissue.

Despite the economic growth of the last few years and the decrease of relative poverty in Romania, the shanty towns flourished, with new ones emerging in and around all Romanian cities. The number of poverty stricken areas is not known but it is thought to reach 2,000, hosting around one million people, with more than 90 per cent being Roma. Though relatively small, the communities are omnipresent and quite homogeneous. This indicates that this is more a general social effect and not a particularity of any region or a cultural choice of the Roma. The disproportionate effect on Roma should also not lead to the conclusion that ethnicity is the only major determinant of the recent raise of the ghettoes.

THE EUROPEAN ROMA GHETTO

After the Italian evictions throughout 2007 and Irish crisis in the summer of 2008, the clumsy French and British policies targeted at Roma immigration are the first major signs of a new European dynamic. Despite the widespread opinion that we are now in a crisis situation generated by the unprecedented wave of Roma immigration towards the West, I would argue that we are just at the beginning of the phenomenon. The apex of the emigrational move was not reached yet and the problems associated are at their very beginning. Based on our direct observations in Roma camps in France, Italy and Serbia, and on the numerous reports about the situation in Spain, the UK, Ireland, etc., it is obvious that we are at the starting block. A natural network is under formation: knowledge, intelligence, resources and solidarity are put at work in order to help relatives and friends to escape the squalid slums of Romania, Serbia, Bulgaria, Hungary, Macedonia, Croatia, Albania and Slovakia. Moldova and Ukraine are waiting in line for the visas.

The general hostility of the Western public and the emerging racist attitudes and policies aiming to reverse the phenomena of Roma immigration are not going to slow down the process. Moving West is the only chance for them. No matter how unwelcoming, the

East is even more problematic: the total lack of social policies, the (maybe) softer but more generalised discrimination, and the sheer number of people lacking basic livelihoods will continue to drive the Roma to places with more opportunities.

The only thing that would calm down the flow would be an improvement of their conditions at home. However, considering the facts and the arguments previously presented, it is not to be expected that a comprehensive policy that would tackle extreme poverty and ethnic exclusion will be created here soon. Historic setbacks like the slavery of the Roma, the Holocaust (Samudaripen in Romanes), and the excesses of socialism are impeding now on our vision for an inclusive society. The current practice of evictions is leading to the development of new peri-urban illegal settlements. Present upgrading interventions in older slums, ethnically addressed but designed without the participation of the inhabitants, profit oriented and never designed for sustainability, are rare (but expensive) and lead to insignificant improvements. Actual 'pilot programmes' are just reinforcing the exclusion status.

We were poor and we still consider ourselves poor, we were mixed and we think of it as the original sin of the communist period. We are now building a society of extreme individualism that enjoys most to mark the boundary of every piece of territory. Whether this is good for the development of private initiative is not the same in the case of the disappearance of public space and in the creation of boundaries between communities. Ghettoes are the expression of this privatisation of the cities by the majority population. Moreover, after a strong period of growth we are now foreseeing a period of recession in which we will have to pay for all the mistakes of the past years. Pensions, public sector salaries and roads are the priorities in Romania, and all discussion, policies and efforts will be directed to that. Extreme poverty has to wait. Roma politicians will be friendly with the gadje politicians, some international and local NGO's will protest against human rights violation, and everybody will invoke the global financial crisis for postponing any action.

Caught between the shadows of the past and the shadows of the future it looks like Romanian society will avoid confronting the shadows of the present. Again and again, it's not the moment for ghettoes, Roma and extreme poverty! Not to mention that there are many who would argue that these are very different issues.

ARCHIPELAGO ON THE MOVE

Mariana Celac

In the autumn of 2009, a local paper reported that the residents of the Gypsy ghetto in the central area of the city of Barlad, northeast Romania, would have to move—it is written—a veritable epopee: "transhipping" (sic) all ghetto Gypsies into civilised houses equipped with modern facilities.

The text was accompanied by a picture showing the layout of the new ghetto: a square courtyard covered with asphalt and bordered by an alignment of identical attached houses with red roofs. Next to that news item the editors made room for the readers' comments. "Why should we give away those new houses that have been financed by the taxpayers to Gypsies and all sorts of dubious characters who will ruin them in less than one winter, the same as they did in the central part of the city?" "The houses ought to go to the hard working and respected members of the community." "The ghetto people should go wherever they came from!"

But where did those Gypsies come from? And where are the ghetto people supposed to go if *vox populi* eventually prevails and the authorities decide to clean up the place and send everyone "home", to their "places of origin", as has happened in recent years? And how and to what extent can the fate of the truly underprivileged, the poorest of the poor (about five per cent of this country's population) be improved in a place where half of the people are also poor, and badly in need decent housing in decent surroundings?

There is one more interesting detail about this piece of journalistic reporting. The word "ghetto" is a novelty in the current descriptions of the blighted urban enclaves. It puts out of use the archaic Turkish word *makhalla* that, with an appropriate qualifier (*mahala tiganeasca*—the Gypsy *makhalla*) singled out urban margins inhabited by the Roma people. Ghetto is replacing milder linguistic options such as *vecinatate* (neighbourhood), *comunitate* (adapted from English) or other words borrowed appropriated from a foreign language: slum, *bidonville* or favela, when a touch of exoticism is intended. The makhalla is becoming obsolete and appears in narratives and folk music lyrics as the last repository of picturesque lifestyles and traditionalist, noisy, insolent, gregarious people, where hedonistic nonchalance and uninhibited mores successfully resist the invasion of Westernising vogues.

Ghetto is a strong word. It now surfaces in the mass media after almost two decades when professionals, authorities, activists and politicians have failed to perceive how common and how critical that phenomenon has become. It is now clear that the concentration of severe poverty in compact areas is not accidental, it is not rural, it is not folkloric, and it is not located exclusively within historically depressed enclaves. It develops in remote, hidden places segregated from the mainstream society, where ugliness, exclusion, desolation and lethargy make the rules. And Roma people are not the only ones to live in deep, chronic and spatially concentrated poverty intrinsically associated with contagious environmental destitution.

Bucharest, Romania
"When do you think the house
is ready?"
"I don't know. A month or two…
I've just started it."
"Where did you live before?"
"With some relatives,
… but only for a few months."
"And before that?"
"We managed as we could…
with relatives and then…"
"So, you move a lot?"
"Yes… Every six months… .
It's kind of hard… .
We help each other as we can,
'cause we are humans, aren't we?"

The new urban ghettos in Romania form The Povera Archipelago. There are between 2,500 and 3,000 islands (no serious census has yet been conducted) with populations varying from a dozen to several thousand inhabitants.

The Barlad Ghetto is illustrative of a specific category of inner city formations, the capital city of Bucharest included. But this is not the only morphological type in a system that displays an astounding variety of particular cases.

A telling example of the origins, evolution and current state of a consolidated ghetto is Strada Dealului neighbourhood in Tîrgu Mures, a large city in the Transylvanian tableland. "Deal" means Hill and, as its name shows, the terrain of the ghetto slopes steeply along a ravine, actually the pit of a now decommissioned brick factory. The brick factory was built in the 1950s to mark the beginnings of the Communist industrialisation programme. Nomadic Gypsies settled there (or had been forced to settle) to became industrial workers alongside some local rural people. And the people moved into prefab blocks of apartments nearby. When the communist regime collapsed in 1989, the brick factory shut its gates. At first, some 60 families moved to the Hill. The community kept growing over the past 20 years. There are now about 200 houses. Almost every new "immigrant" tells the same story: for some reason or another they left the place they lived, usually another cleared ghetto, when they were told to return to "where they came from". They are here on squatted land. So everybody expects that the place will be soon cleared and they will have to go and build another ghetto elsewhere.

In Orastie several dozen families are sheltered under the tiered concrete seatings of an abandoned athletic stadium.

The ill-famed and much photographed garbage dump ghetto of Cluj City was home to several thousand inhabitants before they were transferred to a saner location.

Geoagiu, a small Transylvanian town attracts tourists with its spa facilities. 30 years ago a concrete fence surrounded this Roma ghetto, this was to prevent the visitors from being disturbed by any unpleasant views. As the elder tells us the history, he appears to somehow agree: "You know, we usually keep our children naked because there is so much mud and it wasn't appropriate for the tourists to see so many exposed butts!"

There is a ghetto in the governmental district of Bucharest. On a circular plot of land bordered by an alley where fancy cars are parked surrounded by tall buildings in Boffilian architecture built in the late 80s as part of the last dictator's 'New Civic Center' stands an abandoned small concrete structure. It is 300 metres away from the main entrance of Ceausescu's House of the People; merely 150 metres from the open ground where Madonna was hissed by the public during a recent concert, when she said a few words about the discrimination of gays and Gypsies, and 60 metres away from the entrances decked with national flags of governmental agencies in charge of justice, welfare, housing, local development. Ten years ago, an old man and his dog found shelter there. Now there are a dozen people—idle young men, overworked women, toddlers, teenagers. The walls are black, reminding of past open fires, the only way to keep warm in such a ghetto against biting frost in winter. When questioned, the people say they expect to be evicted and will move to another place.

There is also the Rahova-Ferentari zone in Bucharest. The buildings facing the large avenue have been repaired and freshly painted in invigorating shades of red and yellow. Behind the colourful facades, the once monotonous alignment of box-like panel structures has now been transformed by ghetto life into a Surrealistic urbanscape. The alleys below are full of people and old dilapidated cars, walls are covered with graffiti in support of favourite soccer teams. Those who have the chance to live close to the ground somehow manage to build an extension of the tiny apartment in order to make more room for their large family. Those extensions, which are made of materials to be found in all poverty ghettos, precariously protrude in all directions from the concrete facades and are held up by incredibly frail support poles.

In every large city new islands emerge every summer, while the population of the old ones keeps growing. Newly formed

ABOVE

In the town Tîrgu Mures, the Roma were evicted from Rovinari Street three years ago. Baneasa is a very long street that starts with regular high-rise blocks, flats specific to the communist regime then continues to a former wetland and ends at an industrial area and the former administrative building of a pig farm. The administrative building is inhabited by 35 Roma families, the families that had no room were 'temporary moved' to a container camp which consists of 22 prefabricated containers 2.6 x 5 metres. The average number of persons living in one container is just over five. Eight wooden WCs have been provided for by the city, but there is only one source of water for the entire community.

LEFT

"Go to Geoagiu, people are so poor that they walk naked!" a young man said with irony during our visiting the Orastie neighbourhood. As a matter of fact only small children are naked, quite logically for a large family, there's a lot of mud and the access to water is limited. The two small boys are around three, they are accompanied by a six year old in his large underpants, which is the age of 'shame'. The community leader —also a preacher in the brand new Adventist church—wears a waistcoat and moustache, resembling the traditional Gypsy port. Behind him is an old man in a wheelchair. Old people are few in the ghettos; life expectancy is at least ten years lower than that of the majority.

communities are built on squatted land, settling in derelict, vacant, abandoned or even contaminated and always remote places. Eventually, they will be forced to move once again to build overnight another shelter in another ghetto. The self-generated planning and the unself-conscious architecture that is to be found there develop similar organisational and aesthetical stereotypes into a *sui generis* international ghetto style.

Those who expect to find in the Archipelago islands a wealth of exotic folklore, a quest for identity or regional expression will be baffled. The new urban poverty is uniform, non-specific, highly banal, and non-ethnic. The determinants that bring ghetto people together are always similar: being born in a ghetto, having been left out in the process of economic restructuring and pushed into poverty by a consumerist and segregative urban society. Persistent unemployment, low levels of education, reduced access to jobs, isolation and lost opportunities, the pernicious cycle of welfare dependency and apathy, social isolation and sometimes self-destructive behaviour create and sustain the cycle of spatial decay. The similarities with what is happening in other parts of the world are striking. The facts on the ground confirm what scholars have been saying about the roots and the dimension of the poverty, the failed policies and the future fate of other islands in the global ghetto archipelago, be it a Latin American favela or *barrio*, a *gecekondu* in Turkey, a South Asian or African shantytown.

So, when the question comes to alleviating the ills of places of concentrated poverty, the current philosophy offers answers based on a simplistic deduction: the people live there in appalling conditions so ghettos should be dismantled and people transferred to civilised dwellings sat in a hygienic *milieu*. The professionals—architects and planners—add to that a functionalistic-stylistic approach, most often wrapped in terms of belated modernistic dogma and pigmented with ethno-local formal aesthetic stereotypes.

But when some money is there to open a construction site, the top-down programmes produce invariably the same proposals— either box-like blocs of minimal flats or monotonous aseptic alignments of identical pavilions. Ghetto dwellers move in only to find that the bills are so high that after the first winter in their new homes, the lucky will seek again shelter in the ghetto they came from after letting the new house crumble down. The intentions behind housing affirmative action, subsidies, extension of safety nets and welfare benefits programmes might be compassionate, but their outcome is ineffective and counter intuitive. The decay and distress in "bad neighbourhoods" and the costly remedial plans are following parallel but disjunct trajectories.

Meanwhile, people from the Povera Archipelago are always on the move.

TOP

Roma families lived in social housing blocks near the Mures River on the periphery of Tîrgu Mures. Three years ago the municipality decided to refurbish the flats and the families were promised they could return home. But new families moved in and the original inhabitants were sent to Baneasa Street. Because of overcrowding, nine families settled 200 metres away in makeshift shacks on Rovinari Street. A well was in use but had to be closed when it became unsafe, fortunately friends and relatives living in the surrounding apartments give them water for cooking and washing. Children go to school and some people are employed, they have electricity generators and they heat the shelters with recuperated materials from the neighbourhood.

BOTTOM

The most dynamic and the most visible Romanian Roma community of Tîrgu Mures in the Valea Rece neighbourhood numbers, according to our survey, around 1,560 people but everybody, including city representatives and the police, believe there are at least 3,000 people living here. This misunderstanding underlines not only the lack of a methodological consensus, but also the lack of their community will as political actors.

MURATELLA
ROME ITALY

The inhabitants of the Muratella settlement in Rome, Italy were evicted hastily and violently by the police in 2004. As often happens, there is no time to carry all personal belongings. Here, bulldozers in action are getting rid of the evidence, pushing the trash behind a hill so the passer by will no longer notice the Roma settlement.

MAPPING THE INVISIBLE

104

EU-ROMA GYPSIES

ABOVE

A large awning covered with plastic
sheeting protects the tent and
living quarters of a family.

OPPOSITE

Makeshift shelters with electrical
goods powered by unofficial
electricity connections.

CANDONI IN THE BUSH
ROME ITALY

The spontaneous settlement of Candoni in the Bush neighbours the official Roma settlement of Candoni. New Roma immigrants are camping literally in the bushes. The families tend to build lightweight structures, which are easier to move in the event of a police raid.

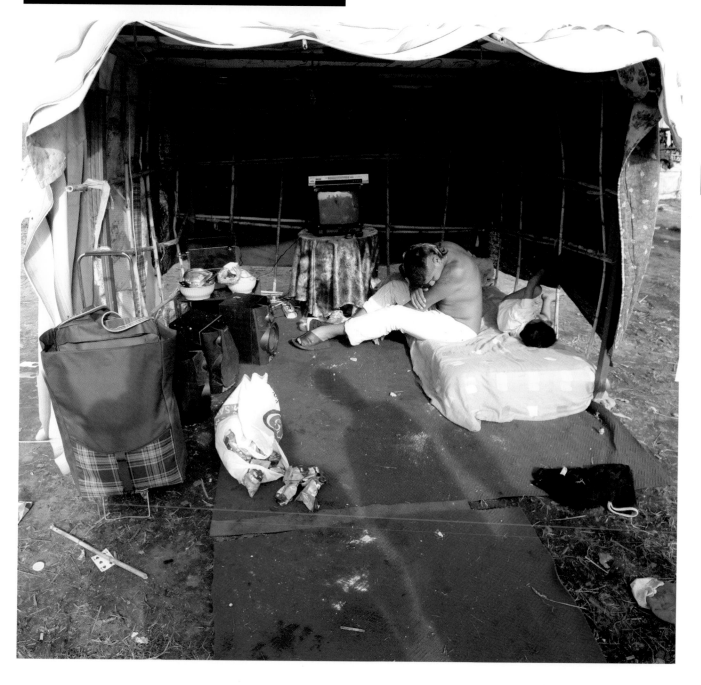

TOP
Makeshift dwellings, private and
public spaces of the temporary
Candoni settlement.

BOTTOM AND OPPOSITE
During the day or when the Roma
are away working, the personal
belongings are covered with cloth
or blankets.

PONTE DI NONA
ROME ITALY

EU-Roma had been notified of the imminent eviction of the Ponte di Nona settlement and negotiated with the families to leave before the police arrived, and to avoid any violent confrontation that might disturb the children. The families originally from Sardinia had been living here for two years.

BOTTOM
During the hot summer, the windows of the caravan had been removed for ventilation.

TOP
Families in Ponte di Nona, before the police eviction.

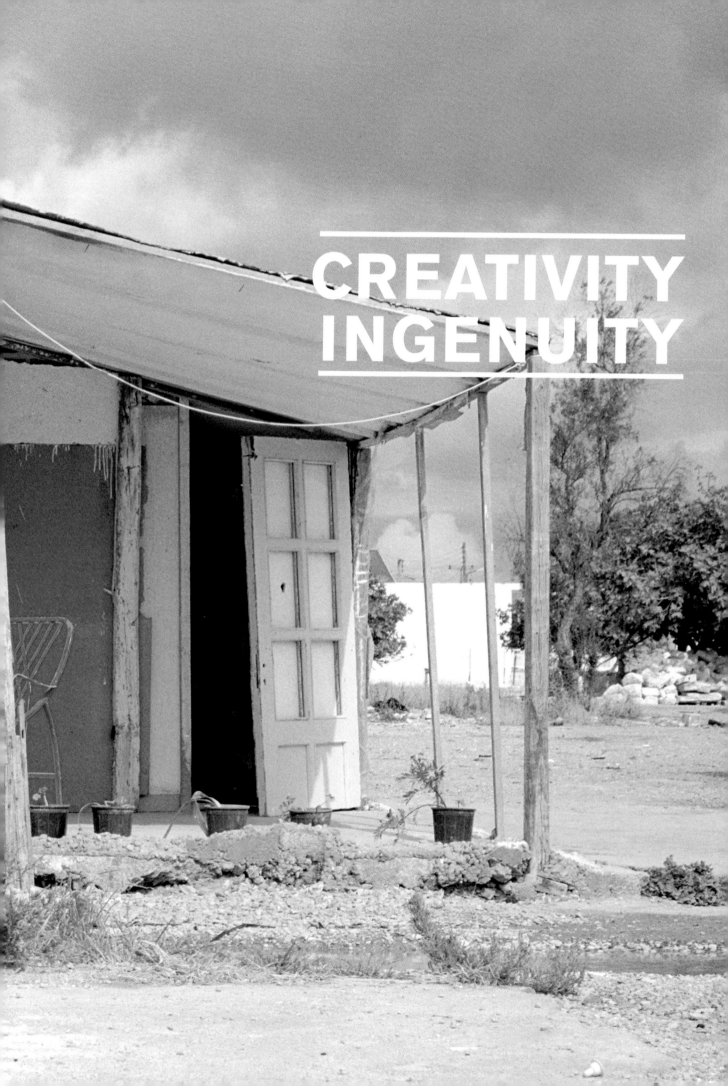

CREATIVITY
INGENUITY

ARCHITECTURE

ROMA EXOSPHERE

Irina Bancescu

From the invisible, but strong, spatial boundaries of the poor Roma improvised households, to the solid limits, often borrowed from local host cultures for the settled and stable ones, exterior space plays an important role in the private and public life of the Roma family and their communities. Roma utilise extensively the exterior space as a living place and consequently it plays host to many of the day-to-day activities, and according to the degree of stability of the families, it also expresses their strong cultural identity. It is interesting to observe this exterior space and how it is inhabited, and which type of construction and objects define or populate the exterior space. This inevitably leads to further investigations about how this space relates to the house and the community, how the transition from private to public is conducted and what story it can tell about the inhabitants.

It is difficult to examine the living conditions of the Roma circumscribed just by poverty and precariousness without taking into account the permanent lack of basic utilities, the impermanence of tenure and consequently the continuous adaptation to an ever changing tomorrow. Harsh poverty reduces all communities, no matter the place and the ethnicity, to the same bleak appearance of desolated shantytowns. However, it often determines a very creative, efficient and ingenious use of available resources. Recycling construction materials reclaimed from abandoned houses or directly from the dumpsite, retrofitting existent structures, using natural building materials such as earth, straw or dry corn leaves, employing textiles of various sizes that are easily transportable and build up an improvised shelter, or even configuring a multifunctional space, are all strategies which form a unique process of survival. The exterior space of a Roma community can be dynamic, continuously fluctuating and diversifying.

The nature of the habitat determines the Roma settlements' spatial order. The contextual influence acts within specific physical parameters (climate, urban or rural environment, topography, available materials, economic conditions, cultures, etc.). In urban areas, the Roma dwellings usually aggregate on small plots, forming clusters that share walls and exterior space. Rural areas are populated with Roma dwellings whose appearance are more house-like and are closer to the traditional Western household stereotype: detached house, veranda, courtyard, annexes, fence, gate, etc.. Often, the urban migration transfers rural values to urban environments so the specific spatial organisation and ways of living are extended and perpetuated in the public realm, emphasising the contrast of 'Otherness' and therefore exclusion.

Functionally speaking, in Roma communities, the exterior space is as important as the interior space as almost all domestic activities happen here and the house often remains an overcrowded depository of valued objects and refuge for rest and intimacy. At the same time, all un-built space around the house is a precious resource for possible additions to the house for the use of a future extended family.

In many communities a large variety of activities take place on the periphery of the built space: cooking, eating, resting, sleeping, working, washing and most of all, partying. The exterior spaces are rarely formalised and they range from transition spaces (various forms of porches, stairs, entrance, canopy, shaded space) to courtyard, which is usually a mirror of the local culture. Various annexes are built from non-permanent materials and recycled waste matter. The workshop is often an annex attached to the house, opened towards the courtyard and producing goods for sale (bricks, pans, pots, etc.) or recycling (iron, plastic, garbage). Making sun-dried bricks requires a lot of space but is a traditional activity that is ecologically sustainable and supports the economic autonomy of the community. The WC is present in the sedentary Roma households and it is a mirror of the family's economical condition: it might be renovated, extended, improved

PREVIOUS PAGE AND OPPOSITE
TAMA Land
Avliza Menidi, Greece.
Maria Papadimitriou, 1999.

ABOVE
This man recently moved into his house in Veresti and hired Romanian painters to decorate his home.

or even in a quasi non-usable state. It is normally distanced from the home and sometimes shared by several families.

Roma households have few domestic animals. The horse is the most frequent, because it is vital economic tool for survival. The coexistence with the beast of draught or burden is frequent; for the Roma transferred to socialist collective dwellings, the ignorance of urban planners and the connection to rural culture has generated strange situations like the horse being sheltered inside the home.

In newly built poverty stricken Roma communities, the exterior space around their dwellings has little vegetation. The courtyard is kept spotless and gives the impression of emptiness and there are few vegetable plots, which is not surprising when further research is conducted. On the one hand, a significant percentage of rural Roma have limited gardening skills, unless they manage to integrate in rural communities and decrease their transitory lifestyle; on the other, the sites where Roma have actually been permitted to build are mostly barren, contaminated former industrial land or have been exposed to various natural hazards such as flood or landslide risk. On entering these communities, the pollution of land, water and even air is flagrant, especially when its a post-industrial infested land. Grime is present in and around the dwellings making the exterior space completely insalubrious. The interior then becomes a clean, ordered and highly decorated refuge in complete contrast to the shocking, miserable and desolated landscape.

Exterior spatial order is also generated by the hand-fabricated structures that populate it. The sunshade installations are basic because they use propped up poles and cloth. Various pieces of old furniture make up improvised eating and resting places. Playgrounds are everywhere and toys are usually scattered over the courtyard as in a living room. The water source, if it exists, is situated centrally and is connected with the laundry space and improvised drainage. The transport means occupy important positions in relation to the dwelling and sometimes provide delimitations and shade for the outside activities.

Symbols of identity or social status such as aesthetic facade and roof treatments, names of the owner written on various parts of the house, protected trees or household shrines or decorative balustrades are present in Roma settlements that have reached a certain degree of stability and comfort. In the extreme case of the evicted families, the whole inventory of the household can be on display in the exterior space.

The settlements' spatial limits range from psychological to physical ones, materialised in constructions, objects, greenery, fence or walls and expressing certain types of social relations. For nomads, the limits of the property are irrelevant; it is a sedentary life that determines the delimitation of borders. Less fortunate households have weaker boundaries that are invisible, but present and functioning, and generate a continuous though divided exterior space. The solid edges are represented by fences, which

are most of the times improvised from recycled materials. For the wealthy Roma, gates and fences are the expression of the social status of the owner, like the examples from Sintesti in Romania.

Textile materials are always accessible and the easiest modality to define and construct exterior space of Roma houses and, generally speaking, they are a characteristic feature of the household. Clothes are usually recycled and ingeniously utilised and they become elements of construction and finishing. Textiles as shutters against voids directly participate in a colourful 'Pop' image of the dwelling in the form of windows, doors, interior and even exterior compartments. Another important role is that of surface finishing. Floors, ceilings or walls become textures and colours, cleaning and delimitating a space with a certain function: sleeping, eating-place or playground. Around the house, textiles dress up improvised structures in order to create protective roof surfaces against sun and rain and act as extensions, complete the eaves and becoming the wrappings, which protect valuable goods cramped near the exterior walls evolving into strange organic extensions to the household. Adding to the bizarre shapes and quite simply nailed onto walls, all kinds of objects inevitably appear: the horse's bridle and harnesses, plastic washing tubs, cast-iron kettles, plastic chairs, bottles or buckets, an old bench, toys, kitchen plates, work tools, a water hose, a bicycle and sometimes even a refrigerator. Finally, clothes and carpets are washed and dried on ropes, fences or any object that enables

BELOW

There is a polemic in the rural village of Valea lui Stan, people doubt that they are Gypsy—just dark Romanians. Although the community share the same living style as Roma, they do not speak Romanes.

the fabric to be stretched, an unfailing image of the Roma dwelling, often in strong contrast with the misery around.

The social aspects are main determinants for the transitional state of the household. Frequently it is single women who care for home and children. The phenomenon of temporary migration from rural areas to cities or overseas distorts the household: father does not exist, mother is working in Italy, many kids are alone at home—the house and its courtyard look damaged and deserted. Urban situations are worse than rural ones, as the slums where Roma live are marginalised and segregated and eviction can happen anytime. Consequently, home and its exterior are in a very precarious state with no public services such as road lamps, making them vulnerable to all hazards and jeopardising a structured life for the inhabitants. Roma rely on the city for social support and black market work, but in such conditions, social integration is a Utopia. The worst cases are the Roma immigrants' camps as these are temporary by definition where the unstable condition is translated into a daily-threatened permanence. Only in the safer and more socially cohesive cases, the exterior of the houses is used and fitted properly for living, as in Salone camp in Rome, Italy.

Public space has a tendency to be defined by common utilities such as water supply, sewerage systems, rubbish disposal, drainage, public lighting, street cleaning, and transport or network cables. As very few of these public services are available, they inhibit the delimitation of public space. The public-private transition is modular and unexpected—public may become private and vice versa and is dependant on the activities performed like a wedding party in a so-called street or just simply a shack serving as refuge against cold weather. The need for manifesting authority inside the community is solved by quite simple methods: the speaker climbs up onto a stone and speaks, therefore conducting a dominating attitude. Public space is generated as a feature and support of an active communitarian life of a unified group of people that follow the same rules. There are special cases when some Roma communities build their open space as a sort of public-private hybrid as in Satra, Veresti in Romania, where private courtyards become common space, 'squares' and 'alleys', where both public and private life melt into a homogenous and united community space.

Poverty and uncertainness generates precariousness in all life aspects of the Roma, visibly manifesting itself in the built form and space around it. The vulnerability and fragility of the communities

is manifested through the degree of ordering and stabilising the exterior space around the dwelling. The more stable the family, the more the transition from private to public space is defined. As a majority of the Roma communities are poor, daily living becomes basic and is planned for the short-term, concentrated inside the family core and is governed by short-term thinking that aims efficiency of survival. This survival also enables a creative potential: extemporisation, informality, spontaneity and self-made objects or utilities are a characteristic of Roma life. It's a story of recycling, inventing, retrofitting, adding, dividing, decorating, but, most of all, surviving.

The interior of an improvised shelter on Cantonului Street. The family had been evicted from their home in the city of Cluj 5km away. The new shelter has been built with planks of woods and covered with plastic sheeting and their belongings are amassed inside.

VERESTI ROMANIA

The Roma of Veresti are traditionally nomadic metal workers and only became sedentary in the 1970s. The caravans were forced to settle on plots of land in rural Romanian villages. There is no provision for planning or infrastructure and the number of Roma has increased creating severe problems of overcrowding.

OPPOSITE

This is not a wealthy Roma home, but the family earned enough to have the interior decorated instead of carpets hanging on the walls, which would be the considered the more traditional style.

TOP

The style of painting could be considered Roma although the designs were painted for the wealthier Roma by local Romanians. In Veresti there is a mixture of traditional and contemporary decorative features.

BOTTOM

In traditional Roma culture, clothing used for the lower part of the body cannot be washed with other clothes. The lavatory is also considered unclean and is always outside the home, especially in the countryside for sanitation reasons but even in the new constructions it is detached from the main edifice.

SPONTANEOUS HOUSING GREECE

**There are five main types of Roma abode:
Houses (conventional constructions made of bricks,
cement, roof tiles); Shacks (aluminium, hardboard,
plastic, wood and/or cement block constructions);
Tents (wood and cloth camping tents) or "Tsandiri"
(wood, bamboo, plastic sheeting); ISO boxes
(containers transformed into homes) and Vehicles
(trucks used for family accommodation).**

**The Greek government has provided conventional
houses for a small minority of Gypsies and most
have happily moved in. Examples, built with
funding from the European Commission, can be
seen outside Thessaloniki and Karditsa. However,
there are cases in Spata Attikis, where the
government has moved the Gypsy population from
their settlements, located near the central road,
to a mountain far from amenities. Here, the state
has installed containers, which do not exceed 40sq
metres each and there is still no electricity or water
supply. Naturally, the Gypsies have complained and
argue that the shacks, which they built themselves,
were much better. The majority of Roma still refuse
to move into the new settlement.**

TAMA Dwellings
Avliza Menidi, Greece.
Maria Papadimitriou, 2000.

SCAMPIA
NAPLES ITALY

The Scampia village on the outskirts of Naples is an example of an urban coexistence with the very particular identity. It extends and widens beneath an overpass of a major street that links the centre to the periphery. The entrance and exit ramps have never been opened to traffic because the houses built block the passage. Unlike many other situations, particularly in Northern Italy, the Roma children speak perfect dialect and very good Italian, an example of their close interrelation with the surrounding Italian neighbourhoods.

Views of Romani dwelling spaces constructed the under the road overpass.

ROMANIAN CALDARARI

Metal recycling is the local industry of Veresti. The Roma make caldrons and other metal goods, and in the summer they tour around the villages in horse driven carts to sell their wares and make repairs, which has become a problem recently as horses have been banned on the main roads.

TOP

The local blacksmith working in the coal forgery.

BOTTOM

The steel rods used for reinforcing concrete have probably been recuperated from garbage pits, children work along side their father for many hours a day.

OPPOSITE

The water well has been covered with perforated washing machine steel drums to avoid any accidents.

CONTEMPORARY ART

PARADISE LOST: THE FIRST ROMA PAVILION
CAMILLA PALESTRA
IN CORRESPONDENCE
WITH DANIEL BAKER

CP　　In 2007 the first Roma Pavilion was established at the 52nd Venice Biennale, with 16 artists representing eight countries. Certainly, the participation of Roma artists in what is perhaps the most outstanding international contemporary art appointment marked a significant threshold. I mean that Roma artists had the chance and the challenge to show their work outside the social and human rights context, so often the only space available to them, and to enter an institutional scene. I use the word challenge because that was also an international showcase where artists could emancipate themselves from the romantic and naïve stereotype for decades superficially associated to Gypsy art. The show was intended as a recognition of individual art practices rather than an exhibition of a collective fact, still with a common cultural framework and a shared social history—as pointed out by the curator Tímea Junghaus (or, in other words, 'multiculturality' as Thomas Acton suggests). You were one of those artists selected. If you look back now, what would be your opinion on that Biennale and, on the basis of your own experience, how would you see the Roma Pavilion in the next Biennale in 2011?

DB　　In relation to terms, although the words Roma and Gypsy are often transferable, I identify myself as Gypsy so I use this term where appropriate.

I would say that 'Paradise Lost: the first Roma Pavilion' was a successful venture for a number of reasons. It gave a high profile platform for the presentation of contemporary visual art practice by Gypsies, something that had not been done on such a scale before. It also offered a new reference point for thinking about Gypsies that was not based entirely upon issues of conflict or didacticism. Art can challenge and influence ideas in ways that direct political action and argument may not. Projects like this show how the Gypsy cultural model can inform new ways of thinking about community construction and notions of nationhood, the potential of which has been obscured by the ongoing prejudice against Gypsy groups that continues to inform Europe's preoccupation with the 'Gypsy problem'. I believe that cultural initiatives like 'Paradise Lost' have helped towards shifting ideas about Gypsies beyond the historic notion of a culture in constant crisis but there is still a long way to go before we see real change.

That said, the project has been highly instrumental in the emergence of a new stage in the development of Gypsy

consciousness, the new phenomenon of the visible Gypsy. This new visibility was embodied in the focused Gypsy presence at Venice and compounded by the nature of the artistic practice on display—visual arts in contrast to the more familiar music or performance based practices that have historically formed the signature Gypsy arts. By its very presence the pavilion highlighted the former absence of visual arts exposure, where any critical discourse relating to Gypsy and Roma visual production had been virtually nonexistent. It is clear then that a new visibility is being formed, the results of which are foregrounding Gypsy visual production and in so doing offering alternative encounters with a marginalised culture. This new focus has come about through the conscious attempt by Gypsies to present new narratives about our community through the occluded field of Gypsy material culture. This new visibility offers opportunities for the re-presentation of Gypsies, a proposition that can then precipitate a re-evaluation of our culture.

'Paradise Lost' marked a high profile point on a trajectory of Gypsy visual arts events that emerged across Europe in 2007 and as such is of considerable significance. It was preceded by *No Gorgios* (London, 2007) curated by myself and Paul Ryan, and *Refusing Exclusion* at the Prague Biennale 2007, curated by James Colman. These exhibition projects set out to test the ways in which Gypsy visual production can be employed to challenge preconceptions whilst at the same time advance the exposure of alternative modes of cultural visibility that challenge notions of the Western Art Canon.

The ways in which these exhibitions were staged meant that they not only challenged perceptions of the Gypsy but also notions of family, community and society structure as well as national territory at a time when Europe's boundaries were becoming more uncertain. It made sense that the rapidly changing concept of Europe with its expansion and renegotiation of boundaries would be drawn to new models of community. The reality of a Gypsy people spread out across territories and with no historic attachment to a place of origin seems unique amongst cultural collectivities. Our absence of a point of departure—in effect a diasporic grouping with no real sense of where our journey began—presents a way of imagining community that is forced to address the ongoing present with less value placed on the significance of geographic belonging. This suggests structures of cultural connection that could be looked to for clues about stability and cohesion in the face of uncertainty that could have particular relevance during the unrest precipitated by the current global economic breakdown. A community that possesses a robust sense of self whilst maintaining the facility for adaptation ought to present an appealing proposition for nations in flux but events like the recent government sanctioned forced fingerprinting of all Roma in Italy tells us that during troubled times attitudes are volatile and memories short.

It is interesting that you ask about the Roma Pavilion in 2011. The 2009 Roma Pavilion was cancelled at the last minute. The reason behind this remains a mystery. This break in what was hoped to be a continuum from the 2007 edition is significant in highlighting an absence. In the light of this it is difficult to say what form the 2011 edition might take, maybe a reaction to this break, maybe a more overtly political stance in reaction to the new wave of violence against Gypsy groups. Two years is a long time in the art world. That it happens at all is the most important thing.

CP Besides the considerations on the Pavilion at the Venice Biennale, in the contemporary art panorama, do you think it is appropriate, or rather limiting, to talk about Roma artists? And yet can we talk about a Roma Art or Roma aesthetics?

DB I think this is entirely dependent upon context; that is, the context in which the artist is being discussed or indeed self identifying. For example it could in some circumstances be appropriate for the artist Chris Offili to be discussed as a black artist. His work employs and explores the aesthetic tones and cultural associations of his own culture and this is partly where the agency of the work lays but at the same time the work occupies its own position within the wider Western art canon and as such can be grouped within wider categorisations of contemporary artists. The same can be said for the naming of art. Offili's work could be called "black art", and again the use of the term is dependent upon the kind of social agency intended by the reference. In the same way a gendered identification of art and artists has its uses but one needs to be wary of the limitations of such classifications. There are some lessons here to be learned from the difficulties that identity politics has encountered in the past in relation to oversimplification of issues and assumptions of homogeneity.

With the emergence of a visual presence for Roma it is understandable that categorisations begin to emerge but these need to be treated cautiously. The appeal of terms like Gypsy Art or Roma Art is easy to understand if attempting to sum up a phenomenon in a phrase, but such phrases are inevitably problematic. Roma Art, the term widely used since the occurrence of the Roma Pavilion in Venice 2007, clearly has many possible meanings any of which may be relevant at any particular time. It is important, therefore, to acknowledge its potential to produce multiple readings and as such the possibility for misinterpretation. Unless reflexively applied and understood, such classification can limit the potentiality of the works and thereby adversely affect their reading. This can then impact on their status as art objects, and could be an effective mechanism for exclusion from the broader contemporary art canon. It is important to be clear about our use of words and, more to the point, to acknowledge the power of naming, and the possibly limiting effects of categorisation on how works of art might be viewed in the light of such labelling.

In the case like the Roma Pavilion the focus on the origins of the makers was important. In this context an initiative can seek to redress the imbalance in the way that works from a particular group have been previously understood. But by privileging this, we are inevitably saying less about the works and more about the makers. The ethnicity of the maker is only one factor in the makeup of any artwork, a factor that can be fore-grounded or otherwise depending on the emphasis desired. As a common linking factor at events like the Venice Biennale this can be seen as important given its historic focus on national territories, but it is the subversion of this categorisation that is one of the major achievements of the pavilion. By questioning the hierarchy of the structures and mechanisms of events like the Biennale we allow a further questioning of the nature of labelling and presupposition—not only by those outside our communities but also from within. Does this bring a wider public any closer to an understanding of the Gypsy community? I think that inevitably it does but this was not necessarily the only intention of the Pavilion. Attempts at understanding, recognition and negotiation across Gypsy communities are equally as important as the development of new avenues of communication with non-Gypsies (*gorgios*). This expansive approach could be a crucial factor in the movement towards shifts in perception allowing the evolution of a community that can actively influence the shaping of its own cultural identity.

CP Considering again the specific case of the Venice Biennale, which is historically based upon the concept of Nation and National Art, artists are called upon to represent their country and meant to convey through their work a common sense of belonging to historical, geographical, political and social context. Undoubtedly the Roma pavilion represented the first truly European pavilion in the Biennale's history. This conception of a transnational pavilion might raise a wider debate on the meaning of a national based structure in a globalised world—and we do not refer just to the art world, and on the notion of a new flexible, 'liquid' identity. A tradition of Roma becomes an innovation for Europe we could dare to say. As a British Roma citizen and as a contemporary artist how do you consider your identity? In international art exhibitions, like the Venice Biennale but not only, are you proud to be there as an artist, as a Roma, or is it simply meaningless to talk about two separate components? How has this been, and still is, influential or even determining in your artistic research and practice, your belonging to a collective identity, the Roma?

PREVIOUS PAGE
Roma Preview Pavilion Bucharest
(Lucy + Jorge Orta), installed in Unirii Plaza and the MNAC (National Museum for Contemporary Art) in October 2008. Touring to the Muzeul Taranului Roman (Museum of traditional culture) in March 2009.

ABOVE
Mirrored Books
Daniel Baker, 2008
Various dimensions
Mixed media on Perspex.

OPPOSITE
Bird Looking Glass
Daniel Baker, 2008
35 x 45 cm
Mixed media on glass.

DB   To echo a point I made earlier in relation to Roma art and artists, my identity shifts depending on the context that I find myself in. I think that this will be the case for everyone no matter where they come from. We all deal with multiple demands upon our attention, which require our subsequent repositioning in relation to them. To be fixed in our position would be limiting and evolution tells us that it is often fatal. Adaptation is a fact of survival and the Gypsy has always displayed an adept facility for this. That said, our experience of the world, which will include our ethnicity and reactions to it, will inevitably inform our choices and actions.

I think that most artists make work in order to make sense of their life. So in answer to your question my work deals with my own experience of the world. This experience is of course informed by my own Gypsy upbringing, my community associations, cultural and political struggles and the subsequent critique thereof. My current research, in which my studio works play a major role, deals primarily with the role that visuality has played in my understanding of the world. This being the case, my focus has fallen upon the unpacking of what could be termed Gypsy aesthetics and the social agency contained therein. This research has come about as a result of my growing recognition of the lack of any substantial study or documentation of visual culture produced by Gypsies and Travellers in the UK. This lack of awareness of Gypsy visuality is echoed in the historic lack of any image of Gypsiness that is not reliant upon stereotyped characterisations. This absence of the 'real' Gypsy has resulted in the lack of any focused cultural agency between Gypsy and non-Gypsy communities and these observations, along with my own experience as a member of a Gypsy community, have lead me to suggest that there is a direct connection between cultural visibility and cultural agency in this case. This attempt to locate meaning within a specific visual culture forms the basis of my current art practice and research.

CP   This publication can be considered one of the results of an international partnership called EU-Roma formed by a group of architects, designers and artists wishing to raise awareness to the cultural diversity and richness of the Roma people. An activist dimension underscored the work of the EU-Roma partners, particularly as a new wave of racial tensions spiralled in Italy and Greece throughout 2008 and 2009. But also the UK was not exempt: if we think about the alarming episodes such as the racial attack on Roma in Belfast, June 2009. What is your experience with Roma communities in the UK and across Europe? From your perspective, which is both of an art world insider and of a Roma community member, do you believe in the productive efficacy of cultural initiatives to create a social debate?

DB   I have previously been involved more directly with Gypsy politics in the UK and Europe. There is I believe a great willingness to move together and towards making positive change for Gypsies and there are important developments occurring. Along with these advancements there are also extremely disturbing events on the rise. Although the will and action is there to tackle the continuing racism and marginalisation of Gypsies across Europe, the comparatively fractured nature of Gypsy politics makes progress slower than it night be if the various political groups could find a more effective way of working more closely together. Gypsies are not alone in this, it is surely the nature of the political

ABOVE
Rose Looking Glass
Daniel Baker, 2008
35 x 45 cm
Mixed media on glass.

OPPOSITE
Surveillance Blanket
Daniel Baker, 2008
400 x 500 cm
Mixed media on polythene.

process but Gypsy politics are possibly unique in their attempt to organise and unify across countries and as well as continents and the challenges that arise from this situation make mobilisation an extremely complex task the challenges of which are often overlooked. Perhaps on a more manageable level cultural initiatives can certainly create social debate, whether these debates effect change in real terms for the communities in question is a different matter. How we translate theoretical positionings and arguments into influential affects are crucial questions in terms of the value of social debate, points, which of course have parallels in the political realm.

CP   In 2007 you co-curated a show in London of works by Gypsies and Travellers, as you mentioned above. What did you intend to achieve with this project? If you had to review that event, do you think it actually had repercussions on the artists involved, the public institutions, the Roma community and the 'ordinary' people?

DB   The exhibition that you refer to was called 'No Gorgios' and was co-curated with fellow artist and researcher Paul Ryan. The show presented work by Gypsies and Travellers in the UK, exhibiting works by makers identified during fieldwork carried out in 2006. The project attempted to open up questions of cultural visibility though an examination of the use of visuality within Gypsy communities. The intention was to increase visibility for Gypsies and offer new access to Gypsy culture. This was achieved by presenting works by Gypsies and Travellers in a contemporary art gallery setting, or outside the usual context that one might usually find them. By so doing the exhibition

intended a presentation of objects that could operate at a position between areas of discourse thereby offering alternatives to the anthropological gaze of Folk Art, the pathologised artefact of Outsider Art and the elitist institutional positioning of Contemporary Art. Inevitably these positionings overlapped and shifted throughout ones experience of the works and as such the project was able to give a viewing experience that challenged the confining nature of the ethnographic exhibit as well as offering a timely alternative to the conspicuous absence of any such previous account of Gypsy visual culture.

The exhibition gave those involved the opportunity to consider their work in a different way. The majority of the makers had not shown their work in a gallery setting before. For them it offered a new way of experiencing the work and the possibility of seeing how different kinds of value may be placed on it. These new values might include how the manufacture of the work can give insight into the economic context or functional uses of the work in relation to their ornamental qualities or the way that a maker might be moved to consider their work within the context of the art world in contrast to the domestic realm. These are useful outcomes. The sale of works is another more tangible outcome and that some of the works were purchased by collections is a more concrete way of quantifying the project's impact on institutional structures and the scope of their curatorial rationale. Some of the works were selected to appear at the Prague Biennale 2007 and subsequent commercial contemporary art presentations.

The catalogue for the show has enjoyed international dissemination through horse fairs and Gypsy festivals as well as conferences, contemporary art galleries, museums and community circulation. This document was the first publication

Sign Works
Daniel Baker, 2009
180 x 60 cm each
Mixed media on Perspex.

about Gypsy visual arts by and for the community in the UK and as such can be seen as an important stage in the development of a discourse surrounding Gypsy visual culture.

CP   With his revolutionary concept of Social Sculpture, Joseph Beuys stated that every one of us is called upon to shape the form of the society in which we live, the future social order. "Images can tell new stories", you stated during a round table in Venice in 2007. Do you believe in art as a tool for social investigation and active participation? What do you think is the role of an artist in our contemporary world? And of a Roma artist?

DB   I certainly believe in art as a tool for social investigation and participation and my current research attempts to engage on both these levels. My studio practice, along with my curating and writing, sets out to determine the ways in which Gypsy visual production has been instrumental in creating and maintaining the current marginalised positioning for Gypsies. So at present my practice as an artist can be seen as a vehicle through which to gain greater understanding of the meaning embedded within Gypsy visual production.

I think that any artist's work reflects their own specific position no matter what their ethnicity. We are, after all, experiencing the world from our own particular standpoint. In this sense the artist who is Roma or Gypsy has a significant contribution to make in terms of giving an account of the world from a Gypsy perspective, one that can be counted alongside and contrasted with the experience of others. Maybe the role of artists then is to offer reflection upon these positions in order to affect an intended outcome through the artwork. This can be thought of as the transmission of the social agency of the artist through the artwork. This question has expansive possibilities and I think that everyone would have a different answer. Every artist has his own reasons for making work. I can only speak about my own intentions, which are currently to gain a greater insight and exposure for my community through the study, theorisation and dissemination of Gypsy visual material culture. The personal dimension of the research means that as I gain greater understanding of the subject matter I also gain greater understanding of myself and of my position in relation to the questions that arise during my practice.

TOP
Anagram Looking Glass
Daniel Baker, 2007
90 x 120 cm
Mixed media on Perspex.

BOTTOM
Suspect Series, right index
Daniel Baker, 2009
110 x 90 cm
Mixed media on Perspex.

ROMA PREVIEW PAVILION
11TH VENICE ARCHITECTURE BIENNALE 2008

Catalin Berescu and EU-Roma

The first Roma Preview Pavilion, presented at the 11th Venice Architecture Biennale, *Out There: Architecture beyond Building* is a travelling forum with the aim of discussing the possible representation of the Roma in future Biennales.

EU-Roma hoped to introduce the idea of a permanent Roma Pavilion at the Biennale. In order to be more than a punctual intervention and to open the way for a solid representation of this European minority for future shows, the pavilion focussed upon Roma as a virtual and global nation and of the housing conditions experienced by Roma in contemporary Europe.

In the context of the extraordinary diversity of Roma groups, it would be an impossible task to illustrate all the values of the sub-ethnic groups, national representatives and activists or any artists or researchers groups. Instead, the Roma Preview Pavilion aims to represent dilemmas and specific topics in an honest way, while accepting the limits of such an enterprise.

ROMA REPRESENTATION

The idea of Roma as a nation has its own difficulties due to the wide diversity of populations, world-wide spread, state of origin, differences in language and customs, social status, trades, etc.. The very idea of a nation is today a regressive concept. An accurate representation of this diversity cannot be built within a single pavilion but in time, with a continuous presence of Roma at international events, thus covering both diversity and geographical spread.

A 'national' Roma pavilion is a provocative idea that could function as an embassy for Roma people. Roma are not militating for a nation state. They seek equal rights in the states in which they live, where policies addressing integration often erase identity and those fostering tradition often maintain underdevelopment. These polar scenarios are a fundamental issue for contemporary Roma and for the programme of the Pavilion.

ROMA IS A VIRTUAL GLOBAL NATION

Contemporary architecture is global. Today's Biennale tends toward individual countries presenting original research or projects, which address the curatorial themes of the wider show. The need to 'represent' the particular nation is replaced by relevance to theme and ability to contribute to a debate.

The theme for this year's Biennale was 'architecture beyond building'. The Roma way of life, with its tense and provocative relationship to the built environment, has significant potential to open an original perspective on this theme. Due to their particular territorial situation Roma are able to skip the historical stage of representation and jump to the stage of being a partner in a relevant global debate. Identity, discrimination, housing rights and public policies for architecture are global themes but also strongly connected to the Roma situation.

A ROMA PAVILION CAN BE A PLACE TO DEBATE GLOBAL ISSUES

It is hoped that the Pavilion will stimulate the creativity of Roma architects struggling to recuperate their identity whilst engaging in an emerging culture of architects and urban planners with an interest in Roma issues and achievements.

This emerging culture is designing and advocating for Roma, whilst in the better instances facilitating and empowering Roma skills, diversity and knowledge, and learning profound lessons. The Pavilion should promote and engage with this dialogue.

FOR ROMA, WITH ROMA!

Often the idea of an archetypal Roma dwelling leads to an exhibition about caravans, tents, 'kastello' and shacks. While aware of these architectural typologies, the Preview Pavilion concentrates on the realities and specificity of the Roma way of life and their everyday struggle to survive, on the limits of the idea of architecture.

OPPOSITE
Roma Preview Pavilion Venice
(Lucy + Jorge Orta), installed in the Giardini for the 11th International Architecture Exhibition of La Biennale di Venezia in September 2008.

BELOW

Roma Preview Pavilion Bucharest
(Lucy + Jorge Orta), installed in
Unirii Plaza and the MNAC (National
Museum for Contemporary Art)
in October 2008. Touring to the
Muzeul Taranului Roman (Museum
of traditional culture) in March 2009.

OPPOSITE
Roma children participating in the
installation of the Roma Preview
Pavilion, Unirii Plaza, Bucharest.

TAMA HOUSE

"I've always found art in the most unexpected places: in the sheds set up at the edges of a city, in the way a woman wore patterned skirts with patterned blouses, in a sidewalk made of marble slabs and Perrier bottle caps. The Greek word for art –*techne*–still holds the promise of linking handwork with know-how, a practical problem with a beautiful solution. In my work, I have used myself as a means to create a dialogue with other people and to understand *techne* as an active social process, filled with both conflict and potential.

The woman captured in the first photograph sits in perfect harmony with her environment, content, looking forward to the future full of life and brio. She was living in a small house full of misery and I tried to make her life a little better. After four years in the same place I built a house for her, we call it the "TAMA House".

The TAMA house was built in 2004 at the TAMA Land, which is located in Avliza, a run-down area in western Athens ten kilometres from the centre of the capital and very close to the new Olympic village. Itinerant populations such as Gypsies and Vlach Romanians from north of Greece use this area as a pied-a-terre. The nomadic way of living and the particularities of the community gave me the idea in 1998, of setting up a system of communication and exchange among the inhabitants, myself, the art people and the public which I called T.A.M.A., Temporary Autonomous Museum for All.

The owner of the TAMA house is Kyriakoula, my best friend in T.A.M.A. and also the guide of the Museum. Her dream for the last 17 years was to live in a 'real' house. What I did was to make the dream come true. We occupied a piece of land and we started to build a house without any permission. Everything is illegal: the land, the house, and the construction workmen. If we generally say that a home is the mirror of its dweller, then the home of a nomadic family in Avliza is also a mirror of the world in which we live."

Maria Papadimitriou, Athens, 2004

LEFT AND OPPOSITE TOP AND BOTTOM
The TAMA House
Avliza Menidi, Greece.
Maria Papadimitriou, 2004.

WANDERING

Created by Lucy Orta during the EU-Roma workshops in London and exhibited in the T.A.M.A. exhibition at the Biennale de Lyon 2009, *Wandering* is a video installation composed of four projections in which a woman dances to the notes of traditional music played by the London Gypsy Orchestra, making wide, lavishly colourful skirts with huge flower prints happily whirl around. This is a subjective but culturally rooted act, a romantic ritual, bursting with energy, with a sense of joyous faith. Thus the work evokes a shared aesthetic and a collective ritual, the strong attitude of the Roma culture with regards to music and dance. What is striking are the gestures and concentration of circular, quick or slow, spontaneous or poetical movements, always changing without losing rigour; at times the motion of the dancer Simona Jovic is ironically affected. They express the flowing, the virtually infinite meeting of courses, of acts, of destinies, of stories–but also a modernity that does not erase tenaciously rooted habits. If the nomadism attributed to the Roma today tends to become a pretext to deprive them of the possibility of settling in one place and establishing bonds, seeing *Wandering* is like travelling the historical route of the Roma people, repeating their wanderings by recuperating the most vital and fecund aspects.

Gabi Scardi

PREVIOUS SPREAD AND LEFT
Wandering
Lucy + Jorge Orta, 2009
Four synchronised high
definition projections
320 x 180 cm each, looped.

Four Skirts, each 20 metres
of Silk viscose, digital design,
and digital print.

SKILLS

KALDERASHA TURIN
THE RECOVERY AND DOCUMENTATION OF A TRADITION

EU-ROMA WORKSHOP, MARCH 2008

This workshop arose out of a meeting with a small group of Turin based Kalderasha artisans. Our original aims of designing an object for and with the community was diverted towards the idea of working with their inherent knowledge. Importance was therefore placed on the disappearing knowledge of the community, and the idea of bringing new value to the Kalderasha's creative skills.

The word Kalderasha derives from the Romanian caldarari, which means someone who makes boilers and other similar metal containers. In fact, the Kalderasha traditionally dedicated themselves to the art of metalworking.

Alaga and Batho, the two artisans involved in the workshop, have lived in Turin since 1969, and in the past worked together producing wood stoves, which were bought by the Roma communities. Due to a crisis in the production of handicrafts, iron and copper work, Alaga and Batho gave up this type of production about ten years ago. Now, they collect and re-utilise old iron

Kalderasha, family portrait.

objects, and only sporadically do they make small objects out of copper.

For this reason we decided to reunite the two old workmates, during the one week experience of the workshop in March 2007, to work with them and design two prototypes of wood and/or carbon stoves. This way, memories reemerged of their past work as artisans and of the objects, which require their particular skills, handed down by their respective fathers, to produce. Alaga and Batho bend iron as though their were folding origami paper. Their stoves are designed in a way that is similar to die cutting systems. Hardly anything remains of the original sheets of metal, with the remnants they make the circular hot plates in cast iron and the iron supports. The metal is joined not by welding but by wedging the pieces together, folding the metal and beating in nails. Everything is made by hand using simple utensils such as scissors, hammers and anvils.

After studying the models and possible variations in shape of the stoves, the recovery of the parts in cast iron (hotplates and rings) determined the size of the prototypes. The workshop concluded in the courtyard-lawn of the public housing estate in Falchera, in front of the Alaga depot, where the stove-making had transformed the public space into a real workshop with children and grandchildren all participating. The workshop represented an educational vehicle at the disposal of the whole community, where pieces of ancient and forgotten knowledge could be reunited and exchanged. The work site developed along with moments of conviviality, establishing different ways of combining times for working, learning, and doing, thus creating a link between past and future generations and reconstructing a none-alienated aesthetic and social collective.

Alaga at work.

LEFT CENTRE
All of the family are involved in
the work.

LEFT BOTTOM
Batho with the youngsters shaping
the large stove.

RIGHT TOP
Alaga at work on the round stove.

RIGHT BOTTOM
The unfinished round stove.

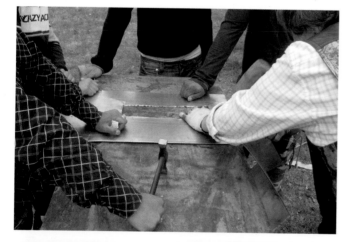

KALDERASHA NOMADES

The Kalderasha are traditionally excellent and knowledgeable metal workers. EU-Roma Italy followed the restoration and plating of a baptismal font. Aldo and Didi carefully dismantle the structure. Each piece is cleaned and re-welded into place. Gold plating is conducted by electrolysis and the object resumes its brilliant original appearance. Young Kalderasha lacquer the font, under the supervision of experienced eyes of the elders who painstakingly reassemble the object.

ROW 1 (FROM LEFT TO RIGHT)
- Tools of the trade.
- With exceptional patience, the original font is disassembled piece by piece.
- Aldo and Didi at work.
- The font in pieces.

ROW 2 (FROM LEFT TO RIGHT)
- Aldo and Didi laying out the fine pieces.
- Tools of the trade.
- All the pieces are ready for repair.
- Welding repairs.

ROW 2 (FROM LEFT TO RIGHT)
- Aldo, the master craftsman assembles the delicate pieces.
- Detail of the font before gold plating.
- After gold plating.
- The finishing touch.

ROW 3 (FROM LEFT TO RIGHT)
- Didi begins reassembling the font.
- Intricate work.
- Assembling.
- Detail of gold plating.

ROW 4 (FROM LEFT TO RIGHT)
- The final sections of the font.
- It begins to take form.
- Finishing touches.
- The last piece of the puzzle.

LUNGO STURA
TURIN ITALY

The linear settlement on the river Stura has existed for more than four years hosting Romanian Roma families. Here we documented copper wire recycling.

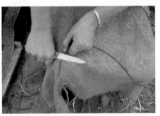

OPPOSITE TOP
Aerial view of Lungo Stura settlement.

BOTTOM
Roma dwellings along the river Stura.

LEFT
Women and men strip the copper
wire from yards of electricity cables.

OVERLEAF TOP
Small church at the entrance
of the settlement.

OVERLEAF BOTTOM
View of the rear dwellings
looking out onto the river.

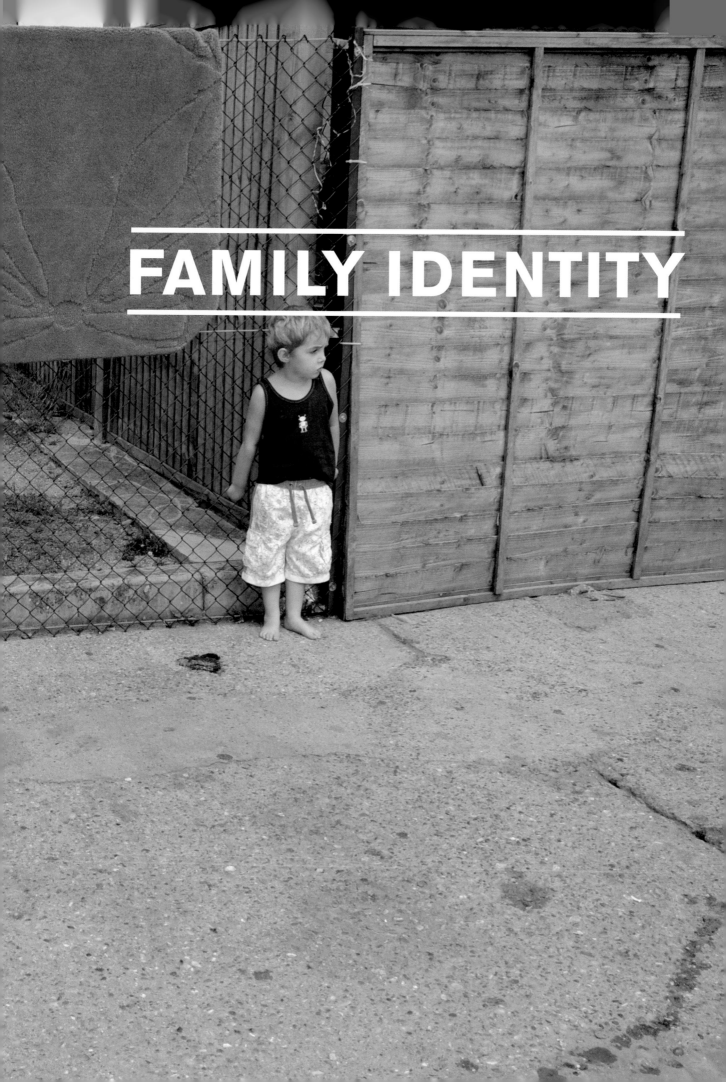

FAMILY IDENTITY

FACES OF CASTEL ROMANO

Illustrations of Roma from photographs by Balo Cizmic. The photographs were originally taken for a film cast recounting the blast attack on Italian soldiers in Afghanistan. 200 faces were edited by LAN, for a series of exhibitions denouncing the frustration of families and their living conditions in Castel Romano.

PREVIOUS PAGE

Holy Communion celebration on Eleonor Street, Tower Hamlets London. Photographed by Valentina Schivardi.

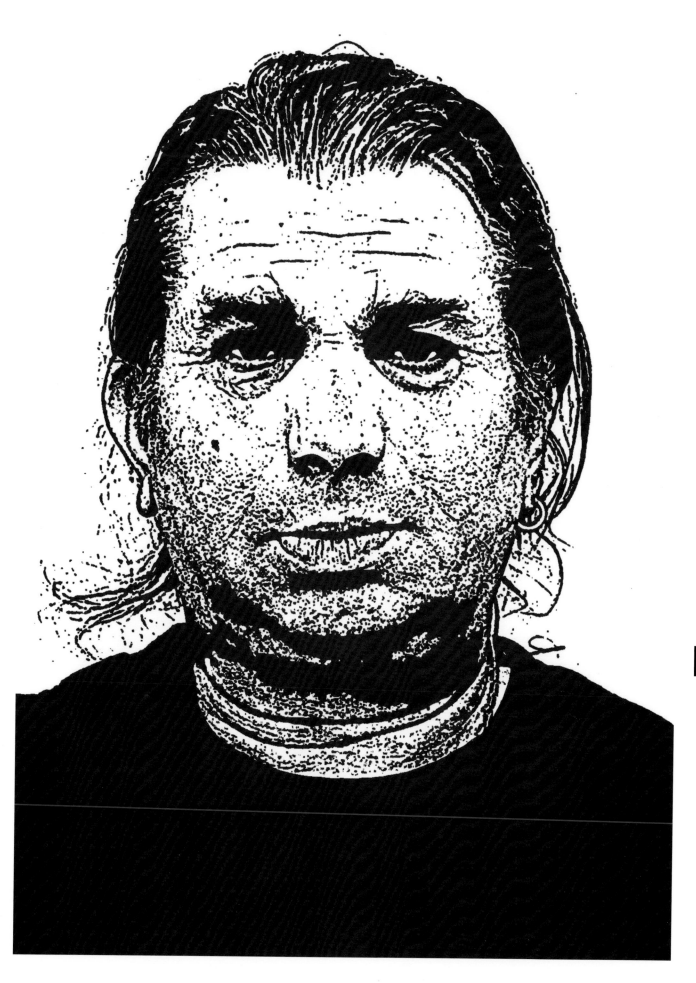

ROMANI WOMEN'S DRESS

A specific feature of traditional Romani women's dress is not the colour or the design of the material, but the fact that it needs to mark the opposition between the pure upper body and the impure lower body, this way being the symbol of purity (*ujipen*) and honour or respect (*pakiv*)

THIS PAGE

In traditional Romanian villages, boys often help their father with craft and girls cook and clean from an early age, in order to become future good daughters-in-law (*boria*). The rules of *honour*, shame and purity develop at an early age and are more visible for girls who begin to wear long skirts.

OPPOSITE

Mother and child in Sintesti village, Romania.

OVERLEAF

Romanian women in the village of Veresti.

GREEK ROMA

It is estimated by the official monitoring reports that the Greek Roma population is about 300,000 although the Roma themselves estimate up to 800,000. Greeks use various names to refer to Gypsies: Athinganee, Tsigganee, Erlides, Giftee (or Giftoi), Roma, Rom, Katsivelee, Tourkogiftee. In general Rom/Roma and Tsigganee are generic terms referring to members of the different Greek Roma groups.

THE FIVE MAJOR GROUPS ARE:

- **The Roma Tsigganee, Orthodox Christians speaking a Balkan dialect of Romany/Romanes.**
- **The Roudarides or Roumanian-Vlach, Orthodox Christians speaking a Vlach Romany dialect arriving from Romania during the eighteenth century.**
- **The Horaha or Tourkogifti, Turkish speaking Muslin Roma living in Greece.**
- **Giftee and Halkiday Roma, also Orthodox Christian.**
- **Migrant Roma, arriving in Greece during the last decade due to persecution in other countries (especially from the Balkans).**

OPPOSITE
Preparation of EU-Roma street party in Volos.

CENTRE LEFT
A family alter in Trikala.

CENTRE RIGHT
A Roma housing development in Volos.

BOTTOM
View of the Roma settlement in Volos.

There are approximately 1,500 citizens living in the community of Aliveri in Volos and most work as traders, travelling across Greece all year round. Out of 300 children 125 attend school, which is a high percentage compared to other Roma communities. Long absences effect regular schooling and although most children finish the third grade only a few pass the ninth grade. With the help of residents, students from the University of Thessaly built a playground using recycled materials. Video: *playground n joy* at www.youtube.com

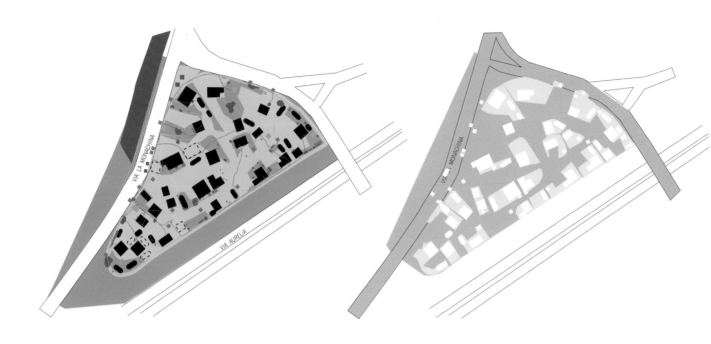

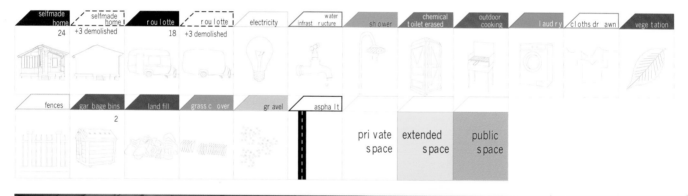

selfmade home	selfmade home	r ou l otte	r ou l otte	electricity	water infrast r ucture	sh ower	chemical toilet erased	outdoor cooking	l aud r y	cl oths dr awn	vege t ation
24	+3 demolished	18	+3 demolished								

fences	gar bage bins	land fill	grass c over	gr avel	aspha lt		pri vate space	extended space	public space	
	2									

MONACHINA ROME ITALY

The Monachina encampment is a community made up of a large extended family originally from the Montenegro. Here the term community implies the ways in which a group of people living together over time organise their common spaces, develop routines and rituals, their ways of resolving and living with differences, and improving their conditions.

What might look chaotic at first is in fact a series of hidden logical patterns. Invisible contracts and divisions of personal space take form in the shape of a road or a parking place. Aesthetic pleasures in the surrounding vegetation, flowers, pictures, trinkets and ornaments, decorated windowpanes etc.—form part of the personal details that ameliorate daily conditions, and these matter a great deal. The mapping of community social relations is as important as the flow of water or electricity across the site. In fact the two are intimately related in a place where access to limited resources must be negotiated.

Autogestione is the reoccurring word—somewhere between "do-it-yourself" and "self-determination". Over a period of 14 years, small wooden houses *barraca* (shacks) have been built and rebuilt many times by their owners, enlarging or diminishing but each time ameliorating. Improvements occur out of previous errors, but also as skills develop and as the network of resources available gets bigger and denser; a network which includes builders who drop off second-hand windows or doors they'd otherwise have to pay to dump. When houses are knocked down by their owners, they are disassembled piece by piece for recycling. But beyond the dwellings themselves there are spaces for laundry and for showers, for outdoor cooking, for parking and for informal piazzas. Some of these spaces are formed by caravans and campervans of different sizes, which are usually used as additional bedrooms. As caravans move, so do spaces. Though the residents of Monachina are no longer nomadic, there is an element of movement and transition present in the camp, a freedom to rearrange and change which is made possible by mobile living spaces.

The positioning of windows respects family ties. Vera's brother Adriano lives in a more secluded spot behind her house with his non-Roma, Romanian wife Liliana. The windows of each house, front and back, look at each other, and Adriano and Vera often speak to each other through the windows, across the space between. A slot of space between the house and a caravan allows for casual movement between the houses.

EU-Roma: "How did you learn to do all this?" Breno: "You need to know, so you just have to find out. If you keep your eyes open, you learn constantly. I'm always looking, and when I see something done well, something I can learn from, I file it away mentally."

Case study Karen Bermann and Alexander Valentino.

OPPOSITE

EU-Roma Mapping indicating the population, groundcover, layout of homes and amenities in Monachina.

BOTTOM

360° interior of Shatka's house.

Sketches of the relationships between utilities and dwellings in Monachina. With special thanks to the Mapping programme at Iowa State University Rome.

OPPOSITE TOP

Shatka's family album.

OPPOSITE BOTTOM

Typical construction style in Monachina. This is in fact the sauna and bathroom.

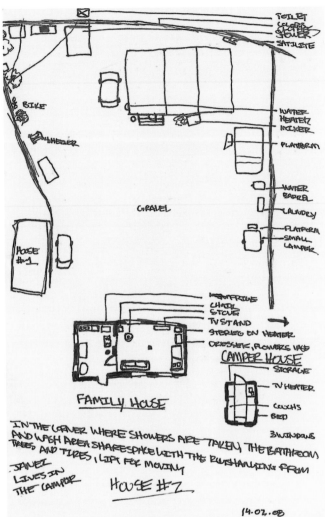

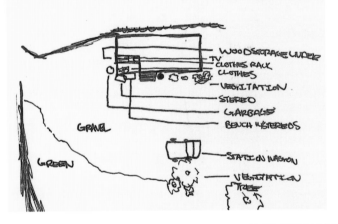

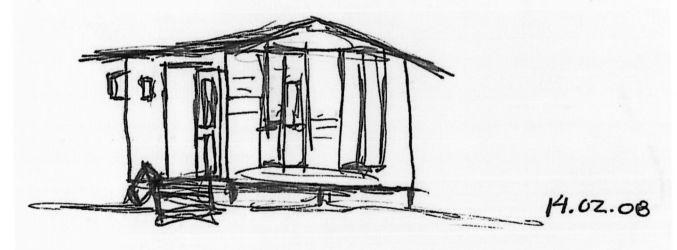

FAMILY MAPPING AT MONACHINA

Monachina is a village made up, with a few exceptions, of one extended family. Our mapping of family ties revealed the relationship between family and social space.

There are two main players whose position both in the family and in space are dominant: the formerly married couple Shatka and Shevko. Duda, another former wife of Shevko's, also lives at Monachina, and the camp is largely populated by the offspring of these two marriages. Within the city of the camp are smaller neighbourhoods made up of smaller family groupings. Ties of affection and disaffection (a son of Duda's who doesn't get on with his mother moved across the camp to live in the realm of his *fratellastri*, or half-brothers and sisters) as well as age organise the space of Monachina.

Shevko's brother, Nego, and his wife, Gemila, also live in the camp and are elders, but are less dominant players; they have a sort of neighbourhood of their own within the larger organisation of the camp, composed of their adult children and their families, whose houses circle around their parents.

Older kids and unmarried couples sleep in caravans, or smaller campers, which function as bedrooms. They are usually adjacent to the family house (though not always; in the case of adults, they can move as affections rise and fall). Thus the older kids get a modicum of privacy.

Shatka, beloved mother and grandmother, sits (that is, her house sits) at the apex of an informal piazza that links the houses and caravans of a number of her children. These children and their grand children move continuously between two or three houses and caravans. Mealtimes are casual; who shows up, eats, and this works out as long as everyone observes fundamental social rules of taking turns. Two of Shatka's grandchildren live with her and an unmarried aunt and take their meals there; there is no doubt about who their parents are, but they are clearly also parented as well by their grandmother and aunt. In this loving way responsibilities for children are shared and space is shared, allowing families to overflow the small houses without anyone being neglected.

Breno and Vera live facing the main entrance to the camp—main because it's where the water source is. Their house therefore functions as a sort of gateway. Vera is the oldest daughter of Shatka living at Monachina. Because of this position in the family, of the excellent dispositions of her six children, because Breno is highly sociable and takes care of many of the technical problems in the camp, and due to the strong cohesion of all of Shatka's children and grandchildren, this house and the adjacent piazza circled by Shatka's house and two caravans functioned as the centre of the camp during the EU-Roma visits. In good weather we met in the piazza, had barbecues with the family. In cold weather we went inside Vera's or Shatka's house. We also used their chemical toilets!

Case study LAN and Iowa State University Rome.

Sketches of the relationships between utilities and dwellings in Monachina. With special thanks to the Mapping programme at Iowa State University, Rome, 2008.

MAPPING | All Layers

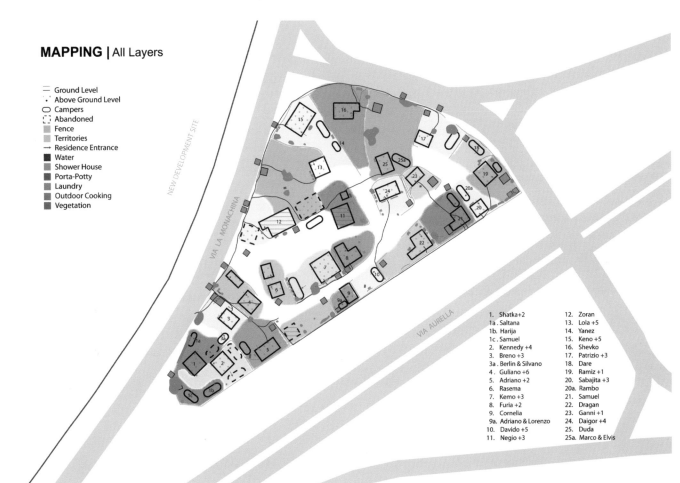

- — Ground Level
- ·‚ Above Ground Level
- ⚬ Campers
- ⌐ Abandoned
- ▨ Fence
- ▨ Territories
- → Residence Entrance
- ■ Water
- ■ Shower House
- ■ Porta-Potty
- ■ Laundry
- ■ Outdoor Cooking
- ■ Vegetation

1. Shatka +2
1a. Saltana
1b. Harija
1c. Samuel
2. Kennedy +4
3. Breno +3
3a. Berlin & Silvano
4. Guliano +6
5. Adriano +2
6. Rasema
7. Kemo +3
8. Furia +2
9. Cornelia
9a. Adriano & Lorenzo
10. Davido +5
11. Negio +3
12. Zoran
13. Lola +5
14. Yanez
15. Keno +5
16. Shevko
17. Patrizio +3
18. Dare
19. Ramiz +1
20. Sabajita +3
20a. Rambo
21. Samuel
22. Dragan
23. Ganni +1
24. Daigor +4
25. Duda
25a. Marco & Elvis

MAPPING | Family Ties_All Families

- —— Parent
- —— Sibling
- —— Child

SOUTHWARK TRAVELLERS LONDON

All photographs form part of the project *Pavee Widden* (Travellers Talking), a collaboration between photographer Eva Sajovic and STAG (Southwark Travellers Action Group), STESS (Southwark Travellers Education Support Services) and Southwark Council.

TOP LEFT

Hazel Walker, Charlene's mother.

TOP RIGHT

Kerrie Wilson, Charlene's daughter.

BOTTOM LEFT

Kathleen and her crystal collection in her living room.

OPPOSITE TOP

Christina, STAG's chair, working at home.

BOTTOM RIGHT

Babes in her living room.

OPPOSITE BOTTOM

Animal in his living room.

TOP
Kerryanne in her mother's bedroom.

BOTTOM
Kizzy outside her caravan.

TOP
Charlene in her living room.

BOTTOM
Martin holding a model cart.

MILE END LONDON

All photographs were taken during the celebration of the Holy Communion of the granddaughter (Ellie), a member of the Gypsy camp located in Eleonor Street, Mile End, London. Valentina Schivardi, June 2009.

OPPOSITE TOP
The arrival of the horse and carriage to take Ellie to the church.

OPPOSITE BOTTOM
Mariann and Demi-Louise at the end of the day.

TOP LEFT
Ellie poses in her great-grandmother Lily's home.

TOP RIGHT
Luis Vuitton party cake.

BOTTOM
Ellie and her girlfriends.

ROMANIAN FAMILIES

To be as dark as a crow, is an injurious term for Romanian Roma. In Southern parts of Europe, where fair-haired blondes are fewer in numbers and racist remarks based on the colour of the skin are part of everyday language, these questions arise from the misconceptions and ignorance of the majority. The presence of a blonde Roma is still an event even though they are not uncommon.

OPPOSITE TOP

Rural Hungarian Roma outside their home on Jigodin Hill, Miercurea Ciuc.

OPPOSITE BOTTOM

In Lehliu village in Calarasi, 11 family members live in this house. Women, children and a young man with a severe mental handicap stay at home and the men work in neighbouring villages. The more qualified can find jobs in Bucharest, 80 kilometres away, for 15 to 25 Euros a day. After paying around ten euro for transportation and cigarettes anything remaining is for food.

BELOW

A young family recently settled on the top of the hill in Tirgu Mures. The young woman is 18 years old and has a child of four. Like all the newcomers they lack identity papers, jobs, education, water, health insurance and so forth.

OPPOSITE TOP

CJ, his wife and two sons in front of their house in Lehliu. It is the last house on the street, without electricity. The single room measures less then nine square meters. He is a stove specialist but cannot work anymore. Typically, the last house on the last street of the last village of a commune is subjected not only to the discrimination of the majority, being a Roma, but also to intra-community discrimination.

OPPOSITE BOTTOM

This family home in Baneasa, Tirgu Mures is inside a container 2.4 x 6 metres. It is also a small shop selling sweets and juice.

TOP AND BOTTOM

Very few Roma still have a nomadic way of life. However this young family with two babies comes from Campulung, 200 kilometres away from the north of Romania, near the mountains. They tour the villages of the Romanian Plain during the summer selling small quantities of timber and return to their village of origin during the cold season.

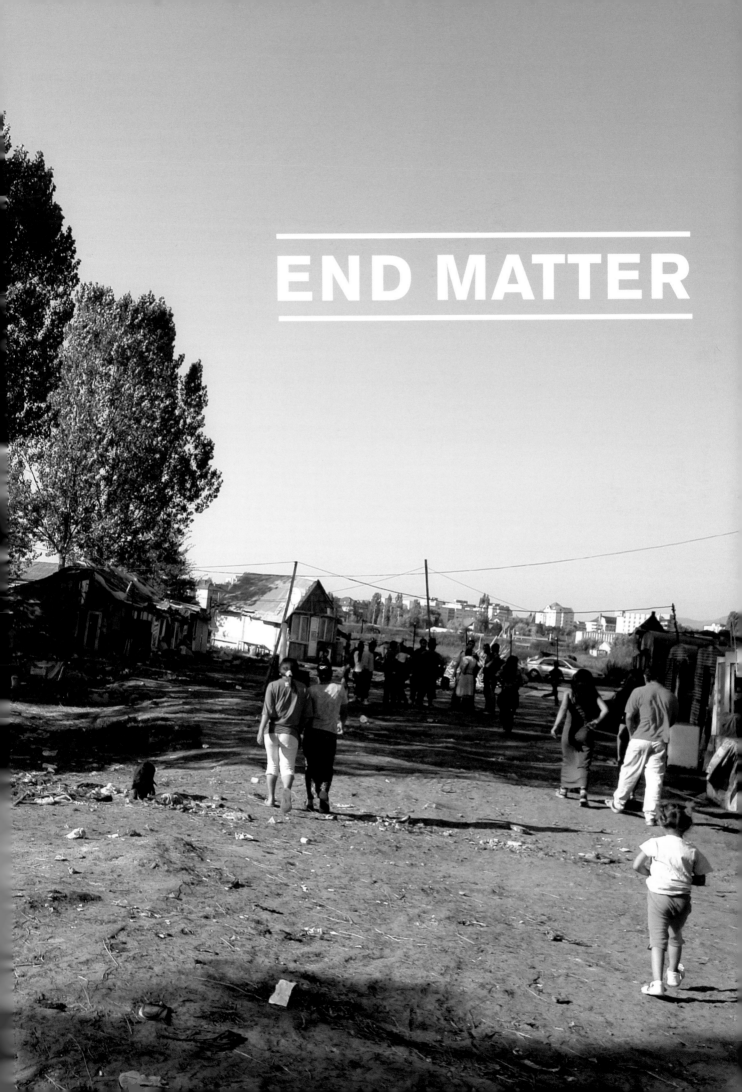

END MATTER

END NOTES

THE PURE PRODUCTS GO CRAZY
WHY ARE WE INTERESTED IN ROMA CULTURE AND SETTLEMENTS?
Yorgos Tzirtzilakis

1 Constant Nieuwenhuys, "New Babylon", in *Constant: New Babylon*, Gemeentemuseum, Den Haag 1974. Rep. in L Andreotti and X Costa, eds, *Theory of the Dérive and Other Situationist Writings on the City*, trans. P Hammond and G Denís, Museu D'Art Contemporani: Barcelona 1996, p. 154, and in F Careri, "Note sull'urbanismo unitario", *Domus*, Oct. 2005. See also, M Wigley, *Constant's New Babylon. The Hyper-Architecture of Desire*, Rotterdam, 1998, pp. 80–81 and T McDonough, "Metastructure: Experimental Utopia and Traumatic Memory in Constant's New Babylon", *Grey Room*, 33, 2008, pp. 84–95. Moreover, we can expand this relation of the Situationists with the Roma culture: "After the Situationist International had been dissolved, Debord's partner Alice Becker-Ho wrote a fascinating little book on the Romany language. There is an obvious sense in which this abiding interest in nomads and Gypsies could also be related to Jorn's support for the spontaneous and the Dionysiac, over the classical and the Apollonian. To be fixed, to be static, is to refuse spontaneous activity, to remain, in a sense, imprisoned in a single, confining location: P Wollen, "Situationists and Architecture", *New Left Review*, 8, March–April, 2001.

2 G Deleuze, F Guattari, *Kafka: Toward a Theory of Minor Literature*,1975, Greek trans. K Papagiorgis, Athens 1998.

3 G Kandylis, *Housing for Gypsies in Avignon*, France,1961, in *Life and Work*, Athens 1985, pp. 134–135.

4 *In The Southern Question*, Antonio Gramsci discusses the relations of dependence in the processes of marginalisation, the mediated representations of the South and the position of intellectuals. In his early *Prison Notebooks*, Gramsci uses the term *subalterno* in its literal sense, but later process the concept to include the categories of the 'inferior', the 'dependent' and the 'marginalised'.

5 C Greenberg, "Avant-Garde and Kitsch", *Partisan Review*, 6:5, 1939, pp. 34–49. The same text appears in a slightly altered form in *Art and Culture*, Boston 1961, pp. 3–21.

6 James Clifford, *The Predicament of Culture: Twentieth Century Ethnography, Literature, and Art*, Cambridge. MA. 1988, p. 1.

7 A Hatzimichali, *Sarakatsani*, 1957, ed. T Ioannou Giannara, Athens 2007.

8 "Lévi-Strauss sees the conventional distinction between 'primitive' and 'civilised' societies, 'historical' and 'non-historical', through an element which was hitherto unnoticed—the mechanism that drives them; based on this, he proposes two new terms: 'warm' and 'cold' societies. Warm societies are those characterised by change and progress, i.e. modern societies. 'Cold' societies are those which appear to remain unchanged, i.e. the primordial ones… Lévi-Strauss… compares 'cold' societies with clocks and 'warm' societies with steam engines": A Kyriakidou-Nestoros, *Claude Lévi-Strauss and his work*, foreword in *Savage Thought*, 1962, Greek trans. E Kalpourtzi, Athens 1977, p. 29.

9 Paolo Virno, *A Grammar of the Multitude. For an Analysis of Contemporary Forms of Life*, 2002, Greek trans. V Passas, ed. G V Davos, Athens 2006, pp. 108–127.

MAPPING THE TRAVELLER
LONDON

1 Winstanley, Gerrard et al, *The True Levellers Standard Advanced* (sic). London: 1649.

2 Reeve, Dominic. *Smoke in the Lanes*. London: Constable and Co., 1958.

3 Superstudio. *The Fundamental Acts*. 1973. A project included in Lang, Peter, and William Menking: *Superstudio: Life Without Objects*, Milan: Skira Editore, 2003.

COMMUNITIES IN URBAN FRONTIERS ISTANBUL

1 www.kiptas.com.tr; www.toki.gov.tr/english

2 TOKI, KIPTAS and their relation to Turkish Government and minister Tayyip Erdogan: Ayse Çavdar, "Tayyip Usülü Kamulastırma", *Express* (social-political magazine), June–July, 2008, p. 22.

3 David Harvey, *Spaces of Global Capitalism : A Theory of Uneven Geographical Development*, Verso: New York, 2006, p. 102.

4 Article 5366: www.tbmm.gov.tr/kanunlar/k5366.html

5 Ingin Kıyak, A, "Sulukule'yi Koruyamazsak 2010'da Neyi Kutlayacagız?", *Radikal*, 2009.

6 UCL Development Planning Unit, 2007, "Stories Behind The Wall: A Development Plan Connecting People And Heritage", http://www.ucl.ac.uk/dpu/BUDD%20Report%202008.pdf

7 Here, we are aware that the usage of 'oppressive mainstream power' seems too vague and general. The explanation could be a state power or economical spatial privatisation (either gentrification or urban transformation), or forced displacement by the state, municipalities (or any top-down regulations, forced organisations that deny, or exclude the participatory practices coming from below).

8 Behar, C, *A Neighbourhood in Ottoman Istanbul*, State University of New York Press: Albany, New York, 2003.

THE POPULATION OF THE SLUMS IN ITALIAN CITIES
AN ANALYSIS OF CAMPS AND SLUMS IN ITALIAN CITIES
Fabrizio Floris

1 Dickens C, *A Tale of Two Cities*, Penguin: London, 2003.

2 Cfr The reports of Naga from 2003 at www.naga.it. Of these, 162 are in Milan alone, 50 in Rome, 12 in Turin (Feantsa 2008, Comune di Milano 2006, Careri 2008).

3 Within the same city, between one quarter and another, there is a difference of ten years' life expectancy (Morrone 2008, p.185).

4 UN-Habitat, The challenge of slums. Global report on human settlements, Unchs, Nairobi 2003.

5 Between the camps and the city it is as if there were a one-way street, via which the city influences the camps but does not permit the camps a similar influence. However, as said above, this is only apparent. Even if the camps are the way they are because the cities choose it to be so, it is also true that the camps contribute to the definition of the city.

6 "The territorial boundary can be merely the symbolic form that combines direction in space with assertions about possession or exclusion" (Sack 1986, p. 32). And not only the possession or exclusion of property (or, really, civil) rights, but also political and social rights.

7 Cfr Simmel *Die Probleme der Geschicthphilosophie* 1905 and 1982.

8 Cfr. Sumner (2002) for the opposition of (folk) society and (mores) society.

9 Lecture, March 2008.

10 As explained, some areas are more similar to slums and others are more like camps in the sense of villages where a homogenous community exists: "where activities and states of mind are much alike for all persons in corresponding sex and age position;

and the career of one generation repeats that of the preceding. So understood, homogeneous is equivalent to 'slow-changing'" (Redfield 1973, p. 9), both in a positive and a negative sense. In places where the main activity is illegal, this activity is transmitted from one generation to another just as other professions pass from fathers to sons.

11 Informal conversation, March 2008.

12 Scampia is a district in the outskirts of Naples infamous for poverty and criminal activity [translator's note].

13 Interview n. 2.

14 It is worth specifying that, in different contexts, friendship and family networks meet up and often there is no friendship outside the family group. However, given the elevated differentiation within the groups, it is possible to find examples where this is true and others where it is false.

15 The doubts and fears expressed about moving into an apartment involve spheres such as:
a the breaking of patriarchal familial unity;
b the diminished presence of a network of solidarity and mutual assistance;
c the risk of finding oneself in a potentially hostile environment, that is, to enter into close contact with the world of the permanent;
d the loss of a physical space in which to celebrate religious rites and social traditions;
e the difficulty of undertaking traditional crafts (eg. metallurgy) or ones linked with the collection of various materials;
f the necessity of changing one's own models of education (City of Turin, 2006).

16 This is an adaptation of a Swahili proverb: "Only the mountains never meet."

THE SHADOWS OF THE FUTURE
EAST EUROPE AND ITS NEW ROMA GHETTOES
Catalin Berescu

1 Politicians are always careful to keep it as low as possible, in order to have good statistics, while philosophers would always argue that the so called normal does not really exist. One thing is for sure; Michel Foucault would have never been employed by the National Institute for Statistics.

2 We should keep in mind that the terminology is not homogeneous and the levels of poverty are named in different ways, but sometimes overlapping and adding some confusion. For example severe poverty is sometimes named extreme while extreme is called absolute. Food poverty is another term used for the bottom level. But generally speaking, the threefold

division is the most popular among researchers. If we are to ever understand poverty, the distinction between relative, severe and extreme poverty should become a common intellectual reference.

3 Although it is popular in the international academic world and it was also introduced to the Romanian public at least from 2004 by an excellent research volume coordinated by the sociologists Manuela Stanculescu and Ionica Berevoescu (Bare Poor, *in search for a better life*, ed. Nemira 2004) the term is not in use in the public discourse. The general reflection of poverty in the political and media discourse starts and stops at the level of pensonaries with small incomes.

PREVIOUS PAGE
Primaverii—Springtime Street, Miercurea Ciuc, Transylvania.

BIOGRAPHIES
EU-ROMA PARTNERS AND ORGANISATIONS

www.eu-roma.net

ITALY

Alexander Valentino Project Coordinator/Architect LAN (Laboratorio Architettura Nomade)

Pietro Nunziante Project Legal Representative/Architect LAN

Nicola Dorigo Salomon Financial Manager

Martin Devrient Photographer/Architect LAN

Andreas Faoro Mapping/Architect

Francesca Rizzetto Web Master/Graphic designer

Giacomo Faiella Graphic designer LAN

Alice Bartoli Architect LAN

Balo Cizmic Roma Expert

And also: **Alessandra Basile, Laura Basco, Karen Bermann, Alma Esposito, Rosandra Esposito, Raffaella Inglese, Peter Lang, Enrica Mattarella, Mario Puorro, Jim Dart, Zoran Hadzovic**

Co-founded in 2004 by Alexander Valentino, Pietro Nunziante and Cristiano Luchetti, **LAN** Laboratorio Architettura Nomade is a non-profit association for the research and diffusion of alternative art and architecture. It specialises in the research process through a didactical laboratory of experimentation that confronts contemporary urban materiality such as the relationship among infrastructures and built environment; the importance of public space; the role of nature in the city; the blurring of public and private space; deterioration processes of abandoned areas; the potentiality of interstitial spaces; conflicts and tensions of temporary urban citizens; auto-organisational expansion and the non-institutional character of some urban development processes. LAN promotes the development of networks between institutions, artists and scholars of different disciplines working together on the understanding of urban processes through action workshops. LAN has since developed an ongoing series of research projects with American schools of architecture and through these workshops LAN supplies the tools to examine the Italian cities and their transformations, applying experiential methods of analysis and design that challenge students to confront themselves with the European metropolitan context. www.lanhub.org

Alexander Valentino graduated in architecture at Università Federico II in 1997 as designer and activist for the conservation and development of peripheral and industrial landscapes, Naples. Bartlett School, Master Program 1999–2000. Founded, radical architecture projects (RAV, Transgressive Architecture), creation of CODOTUA, space for artistic events, London. Collaboration with a number of different architecture offices (Fuksas, Ian+, Ma0) from 2001–03. Member of Stalker from 2002–05). Co-founder of Osservatorio Nomade (On/corviale, On/egnatia, On/roma), Rome. Co-founder of LAN and responsible for Italian study programs for North American Universities in Italy.

Pietro Nunziante is an Architect and has a PhD in Industrial Design, Pietro is involved in architectural projects, landscape design, computer graphics and scientific visualisation. He teaches Advanced Design at Istituto Superiore of Design at the University of Palermo and Napoli. He is currently involved in the development of "free-source" collaborative designing platforms and participates in the creation of independent informational networks. He is a co-founder of LAN.

ROMANIA

Catalin Berescu Team Leader/Architect/ATU Asociatia pentru Tranzitie Urbana/Association for Urban Transition

Irina Bancescu Team Coordinator/Architect

Florin Botonogu Associate/Social Assistant ATU

ATU Asociatia pentru Tranzitie Urbana is an NGO established in Bucharest in 2001 and since 2007 opened an office in Sibiu. ATU members contribute with their specific professional knowledge from the field of architecture, urban design, sociology, anthropology and landscape architecture to various projects combining research and intervention. The main goal is to facilitate the communication between urban actors, by acting as an interface between authorities and local communities. Recent projects include a participatory urban planning process in a poverty stricken neighbourhood in Tîrgu Mures inhabited by Roma; a methodology of planning housing in areas affected by social exclusion for the Ministry of Regional Development; and the development of the concept and a series of actions for a Roma Pavilion in the Venice Architecture Biennale. Current projects are the construction of a community centre in the Roma slum of Ploiesti and a European study on the degradation of Romanian housing estates (condominiums). **www.atu.org.ro**

UK

Lucy Orta Team Leader/Contemporary Visual Artist/Professor at London College of Fashion, University of the Arts London

Sue Konu and David Knight Mapping / Project 35 Architects

Camilla Palestra Team Coordinator Assistant/Curator/London College of Fashion, University of the Arts London

Project 35 architecture, London is led by director Sue Konu. The practice has expertise in housing regeneration and neighbourhood renewal, it has developed a reputation for sustainable and socially engaged projects, with particular experience in affordable housing including for specific ethnic groups. Project 35 also embraces urban design and community-based cultural projects and has won a number of national architectural awards including a Civic Trust Award in 2006. **www.project35.com**

Lucy Orta is a contemporary visual artist based between London and Paris. Together with her partner Jorge Orta, their work deals with social and environmental issues and has been the focus of major exhibitions internationally including: the Hangar Biccoca Centre for contemporary Art in Milan (2008), Boijmans van Beuningen Museum in Rotterdam Holland (2006), Barbican Curve Gallery London and the Bevilacqua La Masa Foundation for the Venice Biennale in Italy (2005). **www.studio-orta.com**
Lucy Orta has been engaged with sustainable art and design education since 2002, she was a founding member of the 'Man & Humanity' Master in Industrial Design for the Design Academy Eindhoven and is now based at the University of the Arts London as Professor of Art, Fashion and the Environment at **London College of Fashion** and works closely with the Centre for Sustainable Fashion. **www.fashion.arts.ac.uk/csf**

GREECE

Maria Papadimitiou Team Leader/ Visual Artist

Niovi Zarabouka-Chatzimanou Assistant/Student of Architecture University of Thessaly

Yorgos Rimenidis Webmaster/Student of Architecture University of Thessaly

Roula Palanta Team Coordinator/Art Historian

T.A.M.A. founded in 2003, is a non-profit research association, which promotes the interaction between art, anthropology, sociology, history, and environment studies through the production of art projects, events and workshops. T.A.M.A.'s research projects address borderline issues such as immigration, temporary settlements, nomadic and illegal behaviours, at the same time co-operating with universities, foundations, theorists, artist, designers, students and the general public locally and internationally. **www.tama.gr**

Maria Papadimitiou a contemporary visual artist received the DESTE award in 2003. She has participated in numerous international exhibitions including: São Paulo Biennial (2002), Manifesta Frankfurt (2003), Espacio Uno, Museo Nacional Centro de Arte Reina Sofia Madrid (2004), Pavilion of Contemporary Art Milan (2005), Bienal de Arquitectura, Arte y Paisaje de Canarias (2006), Kunsthaus Graz (2007, Casa del Lago Mexico City (2008), Fotografia Europea Regio Emilia and Lyon Biennial France (2009). In 1998 Maria Papadimitriou created T.A.M.A. a collaborative project with the Roma community of Avliza on the outskirts of Athens. Since 2001 she teaches at the Department of Architecture at the University of Thessaly. **www.arch.uth.gr/en**

CREDITS

PHOTOGRAPHERS

Thierry Bal
pp. 140, 141, 142

Irina Bancescu
p. 135

Catalin Berescu
pp. 25, 36, 38, 81, 82, 84, 85, 86, 95, 96, 98, 99, 100, 104, 105, 106, 107, 113, 114, 116, 118, 119, 124, 125, 160,162, 180, 181, 182, 183, 184, Back Cover

Martin Devrient
pp. 66, 67, 68 top, 76 bottom, 136, 168, 171 top

Andreas Faoro
pp. 18, 34 top

Aslı İngin / Pelin Tan
pp. 49, 50

Iowa State University Rome Studio
p. 70, 72

Illias Kambourakis
p. 61

LAN (Laboratorio Architecttura Nomade)
pp. 71 bottom, 73, 75, 108

LAN with Laura Basco
p. 145

Lucy Orta
pp. 41 top, 42, 126, 137, 161

Camilla Palestra
p. 41 bottom

Maria Papadimitriou
Front Cover, pp. 61, 166, 167
(p. 166 and p. 167 with students from University of Thessaly)

Projects 35 Architects
p. 47

Eva Sajovic
pp. 174, 175, 176, 177

Valentina Schivardi
pp. 178, 179

UNIRSI Archive
p. 33

Alexander Valentino
pp. 22, 24 bottom, 26, 30, 31, 34 bottom, 35 top, 56, 58, 62, 63, 68 bottom, 76 top three, 78, 88, 90, 102, 103, 122, 123, 144, 146, 147, 148, 149, 150, 151, 152, 164, 171 bottom

POST PRODUCTION GRAPHICS AND ILLUSTRATIONS

Europa
p. 46

LAN
pp. 71 top, 168

LAN with Archintorno
p. 77

LAN with Iowa State University Rome Studio
pp. 28, 170, 173

Project 35 Architects
p. 44, 45

EUROPEAN PARTNER ORGANISATIONS

LAN
Laboratorio Architettura Nomade
Naples Italy

ATU
Asociatia Pentru Tranzitie Urbana
Bucharest Romania

LCF
London College of Fashion
University of the Arts
London UK

T.A.M.A.
Temporary Autonomous Museum for All
Greece

WE WOULD LIKE TO THANK IN PARTICULAR

Archintorno
Autograph ABP London
BP Workshop Budapest
European Roma and Travellers Forum
Federazione Rom e Sinti Insieme
Fondazione Giovanni Michelucci Onlus
Gypsy Roma Traveller History Month UK
Institute of Folklore Marko Cepenkov
University of Architecture and Urban Planning (ION MINCU)
Iowa State University (IASTATE)
Istituto Universitario Orientale
Kalderasha community
LOCUS Athens
Prefecture of Magnesia Volos, Greece
New Jersey Institute of Technology (NJIT)
NIKITA Palermo
NISI MASA Europe
Ohio State University (OSU)
Order of Romanian Architects
Politecnico di Milano Department of Architecture and Urban Planning
Project 35 Architects London
Ratiu Foundation
RIBA Trust London
Rom News Network
Roma Coordination Center Belgrade
Romanian Cultural Centre
Roma Support Group London
Society for the Improvement of Local Roma Communities
Soros Foundation
Studio Orta Paris
Ufficio Nazionale Antidiscriminazioni Razziali (UNAR)
Unione Nazionale ed Internazionale Rom e Sinti in Italia (UNIRSI)
University of Thessaly Department of Architecture, Volos, Greece

And all our partners and Roma friends for their generous support and friendships

Edited by Lucy Orta.

Designed by Johanna Bonnevier
at Black Dog Publishing.

Black Dog Publishing Limited
10a Acton Street
London WC1X 9NG
United Kingdom

ISBN 978 1 906155 91 9

British Library Cataloguing-in-Publication Data.
A CIP record for this book is available from the British Library.

Black Dog Publishing Limited, London, UK,
is an environmentally responsible company.
EU-Roma, Mapping the Invisible
is printed in Malta by Melita Press
on an FSC certified paper.

This project has been funded with support from the
European Commission.

This publication reflects the views only of the author, and the
Commission cannot be held responsible for any use which may
be made of the information contained therein.

Culture

Culture Programme

Education and Culture DG

architecture art design
fashion history photography
theory and things

black dog
publishing

www.blackdogonline.com   london uk